TH
BECAME

THE BOOK THAT BECAME MY COUNSELLOR

A JOE BLOGGS GUIDE TO BETTER WELLBEING

JOE HILTON

The Book Guild Ltd

First published in Great Britain in 2021 by
The Book Guild Ltd
9 Priory Business Park
Wistow Road, Kibworth
Leicestershire, LE8 0RX
Freephone: 0800 999 2982
www.bookguild.co.uk
Email: info@bookguild.co.uk
Twitter: @bookguild

Copyright © 2021 Joe Hilton

The right of Joe Hilton to be identified as the author of this
work has been asserted by him in accordance with the
Copyright, Design and Patents Act 1988.

All rights reserved. No part of this publication may be
reproduced, transmitted, or stored in a retrieval system, in any form or by any means,
without permission in writing from the publisher, nor be otherwise circulated in
any form of binding or cover other than that in which it is published and without
a similar condition being imposed on the subsequent purchaser.

Typeset in 11pt Minio Pro

Printed and bound by CPI Group (UK) Ltd, Croydon, CR0 4YY

ISBN 978 1913551 612

British Library Cataloguing in Publication Data.
A catalogue record for this book is available from the British Library.

There is an acknowledgements section to follow, whereby I thank those close to me, and I dedicate this book further. However, I need to start the book by thanking the number of brilliant authors, speakers and coaches in the self-development field, whose amazing work I have managed to learn from. Learning from their knowledge has allowed me to create this work to pass onto others, learn more about myself, and change the direction of my life for the better.

> "Your quality of success will never outgrow the quality of your thinking."
>
> Steven Green

CONTENTS

Acknowledgements	xiv
Abstract	1
Introduction	4
About The Author	12
What I See As Personal Growth	21

Guidance on 'Finding Yourself' 23

If, perhaps, you're feeling a little lost in life or you wish to understand why you do what you do. Or you simply want a little bit of motivation.

• Feeling stuck isn't necessarily a bad thing	25
• Try to find your 'why'	30
• The art of fulfilment	35

Guidance To Gain Some Control Of Your Life 39

If you find yourself easily influenced by others. You struggle with the opinions of other people. You blame everything else for any problems. Or you constantly wish you had other people's lives.

• Learn to let go of the opinions of others	41
• Be the change in your life	48
• Everything comes down to decisions	52
• Stop comparing yourself to others	55

Guidance Surrounding Your Thoughts   59

If you constantly doubt yourself, give yourself a hard time mentally or you want to learn ways to boost your positivity.

- Directing your thoughts more positively   61
- Creating positive thoughts   66
- Use positive language and self-talk   68
- Positive affirmations   71
- Stop with negative ruminations   73
- Stop your self-limiting beliefs   79
- Stop worrying   85
- Choose how you react to a situation   87
- Learn to live in the 'present moment'   90

Guidance Surrounding Learning   95

Why learning is so vital to self-development and what you can do to improve yours.

- Never stop learning   97
- Have the right attitude to learning   99
- Tools to learn   101
- Start journaling   105
- Be your own counsellor   107

Guidance To Be More Positive   109

Simple, really — several ways in which you can boost positivity. My favourite advice on helping you to achieve this.

- Be the best version of yourself   111
- Quotes/personal mantras   115

- Be nice to one another and give to others — 119
- Change your state — 123
- Start smiling more… — 125
- Get rid of toxic people — 127
- Do not be that negative person! — 131
- Limit your intake of the news and media — 133
- Surround yourself with positive people — 134
- Learn to be grateful — 136

Guidance On Helping To Heal Mental 'Scars' — 139

This is for anyone who might be carrying some pain or struggling to let go of things. It gets a little bit 'deeper' in this section.

- Let go of past mistakes — 141
- Let go of resentment — 144
- Learn to forgive yourself — 146
- Show yourself some love — 148
- Do not be afraid to ask for help — 150

Guidance To Improve Performance — 153

This is more of the die-hard self-development stuff that you see in performance/success-based books. Trying to get the fire in your belly going and planning your next steps.

- Life balance/goal setting — 155
- Create a vision board/page — 162
- Take action — 165
- Create habits — 168
- Morning routines — 170

- Stop living in fear　　175
- Break out of your comfort zone　　179
- Avoid perfectionism and limit distractions　　184
- Summary　　186
- Carry a journal　　188

General Life Advice　　189

As this book is discussing wellbeing, I wanted to give some of my 'everyday life' tips that I try to incorporate to make sure that I get to enjoy life and I don't just watch it pass by me.

- Play more…　　191
- Get outdoors　　195
- Put down your fucking phone　　197
- Spend time with loved ones　　200
- Get social　　201
- Slow down　　203
- Try to 'switch off'　　205

Philosophical Guidance　　207

Something a little bit more 'philosophical', or touching on a few points that get you thinking about your approach to life.

- Change your perception of life itself　　209
- Life is an experiment　　212
- If all else fails… use the 'fuck-it' bucket approach　　214
- Life is the goal　　216
- Live with purpose　　218

Final Tips And Endnotes — **223**

- The mind needs constant discipline — 225
- Endnotes — 227
- Mental health concluder — 229
- Final notes — 232
- Concluding all pieces of guidance — 234

"The last chapter of your life has not been written yet. You hold the pen. Write the story you want to read in the end."

Unknown

ACKNOWLEDGEMENTS

I would like to start by saying thank you to anybody who has ever supported me in life, to my family, friends and partner.

As well as this, I would like to thank those people who perhaps have been less supportive, as it made me question things differently and taught me valuable personal lessons, which ultimately lead me to here.

I would like to dedicate this book to anybody who is suffering from or has suffered through their own mental battles and to the area of Teesside (where I live), which has the accolade no area wants – Britain's suicide capital, with a suicide rate in the town that is over seventy per cent higher than the national (UK) average.

(https://www.gazettelive.co.uk/news/healthmiddlesbrough-uks-suicide-capital-what-14237618)

I want to remind anyone having a hard time that things can always get better. I also want to remind everyone that we can always steer our life in a new direction if we so wish. You are the architect of your own life and you can always develop on a personal level.

ABSTRACT

Section taken from the YouTube video, 'Focus On Yourself And Not Others?' (One of the Best Speeches Ever) ft. Eternal Explorer':

(https://www.youtube.com/watch?v=IKkpiuPruuE)

"There will be days when you ask yourself, 'Where is all this going…? What is the purpose? What is my purpose?' In high school, I thought I'd discover my life purpose when I could answer that age-old question… what do you want to be when you grow up? No.

In college, I thought I would discover it when I could answer, 'What's your major?' Not quite.

I thought I'd maybe discover it when I got a good job; then I would just need to get a few promotions – that didn't work either. I kept convincing myself it was just over the horizon or around the next corner! Nothing worked, and it was really tearing me apart. I was so numbed out!

One part was pushing me to achieve something, and yet the other part was making me ask, 'Is this all there is?'

These are not my own words, but I couldn't have written it better myself. When I heard it, it felt as if was it was written about me. This is exactly how I felt for such a long time – ten years, to be exact. It also turns out I'm obviously not the only one to suffer like this.

At one of my very worst moments, I endured a massive panic attack on the bathroom floor, and I was found by my mum. However, this was just the tip of the iceberg in years filled with complete emptiness inside my mind; I was stressed, angry, worn out and broken, and I was desperate for change. I had tried traditional counselling and it worked (for small periods), but I found myself back there more than once; I still felt like something was missing.

Thankfully for me, I found what you would traditionally label as 'self-help', and I was hooked. You may see this referred to with several different terminologies throughout this book (personal growth, personal development, self-development, self-improvement, wellbeing, mindset, etc.), but the concept is all the same to me. It is all about becoming better in yourself and living a happier, more fulfilled life. Life is short, we get one chance at it, and we should be aiming to live in bliss and abundance.

It is something I have become insanely passionate about. It has helped me look at life from a different perspective. I am now dedicated to a life of constant self-development. Writing this book actually turned out to be my very own independent counsellor at the time, helping to teach me about myself whilst also providing some therapeutic treatment. I still carry a journal to this day. This is not a story solely about mental health or my depression or designed to make you feel sorry for me in any way, but more to demonstrate how personal development has helped me and the power that I feel it holds. I now want to share some of the knowledge I have learned with you, and I must express that if this even can help just one person, then the whole book is a success to me.

I must stress, I am still teaching myself daily and carrying out these habits; I must keep learning them. This is now a lifelong practice. I am trying my best to continue to live a positive life, and I now want to try and help teach others how to live their best lives... which is what has brought me **here**.

INTRODUCTION

Firstly, thank you for taking interest in my project.

I would like to begin by referring to it as a 'project', as this is exactly what it began as. I didn't know where this was going when I started my journaling, note-scribbling, soul-searching, motivation-seeking pursuit and I never for one minute thought I would be in a position where I was writing a book. As well as this, if it is to fail fucking miserably then I don't have to succumb myself to the fact that I am a failed first-time author (apparently quite common), and I can simply just put it down to a project gone badly, which seems a little more comforting.

In addition to this, I honestly never thought I would finish it! I change my mind with ideas quite frequently, so I didn't know where this would take me; therefore, it made sense to talk it down to even myself initially.

However, I have found a lot of enjoyment in writing it. I hope you enjoy it too and that in the process of reading it you can take something positive from it.

If you do, it's fantastic and a job well done! But if you

INTRODUCTION

don't… well… it was not meant to be… but we can't please everyone!

So what will you find in this project?

- A snapshot of several topics related to personal growth, self-help, personal development, mindset, self-development, wellbeing or any other terminology which I believe reflects positive psychology or to help us live more positively.
- Some of the concepts I used personally (or what I believe to be the best principles) to help you live a more content life.
- There is a little bit for everyone. The structure of the book also means you can skip to wherever you feel is relevant for you, and you can dip in and out if you so wish. I think there are lessons to be learned by consuming all the content. There are also journal areas for you to scribble your own notes and to get you thinking and taking some action. (If you're reading an e-book, grab a pen and paper now.)

What won't you find in this project?

- Polite vocabulary at all times (I cannot help it; I tried writing with a '**professional only**' type of mentality, but it didn't work for me… so if you dislike swearing… apologies… **there is some**).
- How to make £1 million in thirty days or some other get-rich-quick scheme. Any 'magical formulas' to achieving 'life mastery'.

- Any claims of being an 'expert'; even though I *love* this subject and I now use my experiences to help others, I am honestly just an 'everyday' guy whose passion was ignited from personal experiences. I just give you my version on some already proven tactics. At this stage of my journey, I am in *no* way an expert.

Who is this project for?

- Anyone who wants to learn about positive actions and trying to live a more content life.
- Anybody interested in positive change and wanting to be the architect of their own life.
- Anyone who likes reading a lot of good quotes that make you feel a bit fucking happier.
- Anybody lost who perhaps needs direction.
- Anybody who wants to learn about the principles related to performance or perhaps needs a kick up the arse.
- Anybody who wants to grow on a personal level and wants to learn the importance of this.
- Anybody who feels fantastic but still wants reminding of some positive concepts.
- In a nutshell, anybody already interested in self-help/development/improvement-style books or even newbies looking for a starting point.

How has this been achieved?

- By filtering through *a lot* of material already out there. As stated, I have personally fully immersed myself into

anything related to the topics discussed above. I have then taken these from a variety of platforms and pulled out what I believe to be the 'best bits' and a number of tips/principles to follow here.
- Reference is therefore made throughout to several authors, psychologists, motivational speakers, wellbeing coaches, etc. and the content already out there. As stated, I also add my own personal views and experiences to this.

Note: Throughout, I will relate a lot of my own struggles to career and work life, as this is where I was affected. However, a lot of the concepts I talk about I want you to try and apply to any area of your life you feel applicable.

So let's get started. And just to clarify early, this is a *book*, one I am super proud of completing, which means yes, *another* 'self-help-style book' is on the agenda, and it is safe to say that writing this book is not a case of reinventing the wheel.

If I were to tell you my honest opinion… I don't believe much of the content massively differs – well, at least from what I have read, which is, perhaps, a bit of a controversial statement and it is hardly selling it immediately, I know, but I believe it is often the same tried-and-tested methods, with the author's own spin on it, based on their experience. This is completely fine, may I add… because it fucking works!

Trust me, I am different person as a result of it! You're now going to get my interpretation of various methods.

In regard to myself, at the time of writing I am in no way an established name in the industry (not yet, anyway… though I do hope to go on to this… **dream big,** I say… but let's see how this book goes first, eh!). Perhaps this book will serve as a good tool for reflection in years to come, or it completely flops at the first hurdle – who knows?

However, I genuinely believe that absolutely anybody can and should be working on their personal development daily. I wish they would teach this stuff in schools or from an early age – honestly, it would have set me up personally so much better.

I do feel it is important to express that we must take risks in life – if it pays off, then great; if it doesn't, we learn. This is an important bit of positive advice from me: don't be afraid to take risks. I would certainly rather take risks than look back on my deathbed and think, If only I had tried that. I would be lying if I said I had never had doubts about writing a book, but sometimes we must gamble and dare to be brave. If I want to teach others about the power of self-development, I have to be prepared to practise what I preach.

Seriously, though, had you have told me a number of years ago that I would be writing a book about this subject, I would have never have believed you. I didn't even know what 'self-development' was. My mind is in such a healthier place now, which I wholeheartedly believe has come from this pursuit.

I am very much on the start of my mission to help others, though I have big plans. You could say I was working back over. Normally, people would build a name in the field and then release the book. I am releasing the book first whilst slowly finding my feet in this field. I am creating my Joe Bloggs Talks brand (details to follow later). I am determined to spread more positivity to the world, and this all literally stemmed from battling my own fucking rubbish thoughts for so long.

I am stupidly passionate about it now. Seriously, self-development is like oxygen for me now. That's how much I feel we all need it. I have to show everyone the benefits.

That said, I must express, though, I am not a trained professional in this field. Disclaimer here. Try the methods at your discretion, but consult a doctor or professional if you need further assistance, please do not try and sue me! I am not claiming to be anything I am not.

There isn't a 'magic formula' to living a perfect life, and I personally despise those courses that claim to achieve life 'mastery', as I don't think there is such a concept. (I personally will never sell any service that claims to achieve this; I believe in never-ending improvement, which therefore means 'mastery' is unattainable anyway.) Not all the methods in this book will tickle your fancy. Yes, I swear by personal development and yes, it does work, but it's about finding parts that work for you. I wouldn't expect you to take away everything I speak of in this book, but just highlight the parts that you see fit.

I have dedicated areas for you to journal, and don't be afraid to get a pen and scribble all over the book. If you have an e-book, please be ready to make notes. I strongly encourage this.

When I first got into this area, I simply set out on a path to cheer myself up a little, as behind the scenes, I was constantly fucking miserable. Where was I going in life; what was I doing? I had no clue and it really upset me but also sincerely pissed me off.

I am honestly just an everyday guy, or self-proclaimed 'Joe Bloggs', which is a name given for a typical average man, who set out to learn more about himself. In doing so, I delved deep into self-help, self-development, personal growth, happiness-searching or whatever you wish to categorise it as; it impacted me so profoundly that I feel I owe it to the world.

I know this sounds a little bit cliché, but truthfully, that's how much it changed my life.

It also turns out that what started as my personal journal essentially became my own counsellor (hence the name). I found writing about areas I was struggling with allowed me to learn more about feeling certain ways and to assist me in feeling better. It was a healthier escape. I wanted to use writing this book as an example of how we can overcome some of the things in life which hold us back, and I refer to this throughout. I also found writing about the positive content I heard helped give me some direction and stay motivated, so this is something I would highly recommend. Seriously, if there is one thing to take from this whole book, go grab yourself a little notepad from your local shop and carry it with you as much as you can! This is going to become your mind's best friend and your most powerful asset.

If you had told me a few years ago I would be writing a book encouraging the world to essentially journal, I would have asked you what drugs you were taking. However, this is how it all started for me.

I do believe that life is a long road full of bumps and bends and challenges. This whole book is a collaboration of what I feel are good principles on helping live a good or better life so that you can navigate that road a little easier. Even as I intend to teach others, I can often revisit areas and come back to them when I am struggling in certain areas (hence my counsellor) or I can find new content when looking in new areas to grow further. This book could essentially be an eternal project, as we never stop learning about ourselves; I could write about this till the day I die if I chose not to release it.

I want to try my best to make sure that every single person who reads this can take something from it: newbies to self-development, trained professionals, CEOs of companies, retired professionals, locals in the pub or even my next-door neighbour (he might be my only reader).

Important note: you do not have to be crippled with anxiety or depression to read this and learn some valuable information. Likewise, you may feel you have all your shit together and are crushing life, and I still believe you can take something from this. Self-development and general wellbeing are applicable to absolutely everyone. If you have absolutely everything worked out and life and you feel there are no areas you can improve on, then please… show me the blueprint.

That said, on a serious note there will be some topics discussed throughout that I am not an expert in. For example, if you are struggling with mental health issues, I also want to again express that the tips I give are not a replacement for seeing a professional.

I will refer to a lot of things throughout in a light-hearted sense. I am certainly not taking the topic lightly; it's what lead me here in the fucking first place!

I will discuss some of my personal battles and thought processes throughout, and by doing so, I may be able to help others.

That said, if this all goes to plan and it's deemed a success, I am definitely putting 'author' on my LinkedIn page, I will be the star in my local pub and hopefully I will retire at thirty (but we will see).

ABOUT THE AUTHOR

All best-sellers have a part about the author, don't they? I best keep up the tradition...

Now I am going to keep this brief, but I feel it is worth sharing a little bit about me.

Drum roll...

I grew up in a small, quiet town known as Billingham. On the outskirts of an area known as Teesside, UK (mentioned in the above), I grew up in an immediate family of four. I have a very supportive family on my mother's side. I have two amazing parents and one sister whom I am fortunate to be close with. I was well supported as a child, well looked after and raised well. As a kid, I enjoyed sport, and my father would spend his weeknights and weekends driving me up and down the country to play football. I was well looked after, and whilst never overly 'spoilt', my parents never let me go without. I was raised to be well mannered, and whilst never perfect, I did OK. I went to state schools, and when I left, I went straight onto college, then straight on to university and attained a BSc followed by a MSc in Sports Science. All sounds pretty good so far, doesn't it? This is hardly a terrible upbringing. I did what everyone is supposed to do (at least, I thought I was ticking the boxes) and was raised the way any child should appreciate being raised.

So why am I here now and writing this? Why did I set out on such a journey of personal growth?

Unfortunately for me, for a good ten years after leaving school, I felt I was such a 'failure' within the eyes of society, that it actually led me to become significantly depressed.

In the beginning, this was a very tough time for me. Why the fuck did I feel like this? Who was I to feel like this? I felt selfish, to tell you the truth... my background is hardly a horror show.

I could not get my head around why I was feeling the way I was. As stated, growing up, I had a good upbringing, a supportive family (I still do) and I had always been genuinely happy in my youth... So why did I suddenly find myself feeling this way?

For me, it was as I left school and entered the 'real world', as it was often referred to, that I became a bit fixated on what 'success' meant to society; it had me constantly feeling like a failure. I loved sport my whole life, therefore I went to college and studied it, and I got high grades. I went to university, got a first-class honours degree and then completed my master's degree with merit. To everyone else who knew me, I appeared to be going on the right path (and it seemed fitting); however, to me, I just felt fucking empty. I fell out of love with sport for several years, and by the end of my degree, I couldn't even face doing the work. I pushed on to complete it and hid behind smiles, but behind closed doors, I felt like I had completely lost myself.

I thought going to university was what you were supposed to do. Then you get a job, and then you love that for the rest of your life, and everything is just picture fucking perfect. You get jobs (some are just temporary whilst you get your qualifications), then you get your dream job, do well with money and then you're made for life, and this is just exactly how life is supposed to go… smooth sailing. However, I just hated what I was doing; the jobs I was working in I disliked ninety-nine per cent of the time. I was just completely lost in life.

Then the questions started… Is this it? Seriously, if this is all there is to life, then I don't want to be here. Work, pay bills and then die – no thank you! I honestly felt like I didn't understand how to be an adult! I know that sounds absolutely ridiculous, but it's true.

Then my friends started making good money, and I wasn't. Therefore, to me, in the eyes of society, I was one hundred per cent just a failure. I was worthless. I had no hope. Was it me? Am I a lazy person with no work ethic at all? Am I just not cut out for the 'real world'?

Well, let me tell you, I certainly wasn't lazy. At one point, I was studying daily and then working evenings in a bar. On weekends I would also work in the bar whilst also volunteering at local football clubs to further my qualifications. I literally had no time to myself (which, thinking back, was likely a huge contributing factor to my feelings) and when I did get moments to spare… it was spent partying. This was all whilst always questioning why I was doing everything. It was so physically and emotionally draining. It wasn't healthy.

I had no fulfilment whatsoever. In my eyes, during these ten years I had made what I also believe to be poor career choices (because it didn't bring lots of money and therefore what I believed to be guaranteed happiness). I felt like I was desperately chasing something, but with each other pathway I explored and failed to fall in love with, my mood was getting lower and lower. I was seriously questioning myself too; as everyone was telling me, I just had to get on with it – "It's just life."

As I changed roles and did new things, I kept revisiting this loop and finding myself falling back into this vicious cycle of negative thoughts and moods, and this just kept leading me into depressive states of mind. Was it me? Did I just have to 'man up' and get on with it? This is life and we just face it. I come from a working-class town, a place of hard-working people; it could be seen as being weak to be this way. Although I don't think people knew the extent of my feelings initially.

I will not go into specifically everything I have done as a career year by year, as the purpose of this book is not to demonstrate my CV. However, I am currently twenty-nine years old (at the time of writing) and currently work full time for the NHS and have done for the last four years with genuine fulfilment. I now like to spread positive and motivating messages through my 'Joe Bloggs Talks' brand on the side, which I hope to grow into something permanent. I now have my own big aspirations and goals, and I now feel content in my career choices. It wasn't always like this, though; I have also worked in sports coaching, performance analysis, retail, hospitality management, recruitment and sales, and failed to set up a business (there is probably more).

As I job-hopped (some lasted less than a month and some lasted years), I was repeatedly told, "You don't want to keep changing jobs; it will be terrible for your CV." But just nothing was leaving me truly content. I always felt like there was more.

As I worked in a bar, I felt I was ridiculed at times (even though the job was much more satisfying for me personally than most). Then I remember getting my first job in the sales recruitment industry and being told, "Well done for finally getting a real job."

Can someone please define to me what a 'real' fucking job is? I hated this!

I felt I had no idea what I was supposed to be doing and I worked myself up so much about how I was being viewed. I was embarrassed by myself, being honest. At my very worst, I didn't even want to get out of bed, yet I had to… Busyness was a distraction, as was the heavy drink and drug binges in those spare moments.

Thankfully, as stated, I am now finding more 'purpose' in life, and by consistently working on myself, I feel as if I am always learning. I am more educated about my own mental health and wellbeing, and this started a passion to help others. I am more driven and motivated in life. Not only that; by teaching others these principles in whatever way this is, it helps me learn about myself further. It keeps me in that healthy mind frame.

Personally, I now try to enjoy what I am doing right there in the moment more often. If my passions change, I must be OK with this now. I have also realised that there is literally more to life than only worrying about what I am doing for a living (thank goodness I learned this one!).

I am still very much determined to be 'successful', and I am slowly starting to acknowledge I have done some good things in my so far short life. That said, I am determined to find further 'success', but I have to achieve this on my terms. Nobody else's! Doing what I want to do! So now I am setting goals that I want to achieve for me. If somebody does not agree with what I am doing, then I honestly could not give a fuck anymore. I am doing it because at this moment in my life, this is what I want to be doing or seeking. Therefore, I am here now doing this; this is what I want to do.

This whole book is also not going to be a conversation about career choices, but the reality is, a lot of people hate their jobs. In the book *How to Find Fulfilling Work* by Roman Krznaric, he claims fifty per cent of workers in the Western world are unhappy in their jobs, and if people had the option to start over, sixty per cent would. I just do not believe that this many people should be unhappy at work. I honestly find it astounding. It is so sad in the grand scheme of things, as we literally only get one chance at life and working takes up a large part of it. In regard to changing course, the reality is we can pave ourselves a new path if we so wish. This is another important message.

Nevertheless, success or fulfilment are broad terms that be applied to various aspects of our life. I also realise there is much more to depression than simply our careers, but for me personally, this is where it affected me at first, which then affected all other areas of my life. To someone looking in, this may seem like a completely obscene thing to feel so down about; to others, they might be able to relate. The truth is, anybody can be fighting a personal battle. Some we can relate to, some would make no sense at all and unfortunately, we won't even hear about some, as sadly, it is sometimes too late.

One thing, though: had this all not happened, I may never have set out on this path of personal development. So for this, I must be grateful, for this is a path that I feel will serve me more in my life going forward than any job or career choice ever could.

I truly believe self-development is an ongoing progression of life, and without it you just stay still. It's the true route to happiness to try and be the best 'you' that you can be.

This obviously is just my opinion, but like I say, I do wish they had taught me these skills in school, as it would have much better prepared me for the 'real world'.

In some strange sort of way, I feel I owe my life to the concept of personal growth, which is why I am so passionate about it. I want to share as much of what I know with others. To re-emphasise this, I live by the motto that if just one thing resonates with someone, then it's a job well done.

I also now understand that the past is all just part of my journey. I might have made some different decisions looking back, but now these decisions have been made and cannot be changed (here is another little pointer for the reader: the past **cannot** be changed). I also must be grateful for the skills I have learned throughout my life thus far.

I have been fortunate to learn a lot of skills on the way. However, the most enjoyment I get from any of the above has been putting the time and effort into developing me personally (in case you haven't realised yet), which I now do every single day.

I truly believe that by working on you, you get a sense of personal achievement and can continually grow as a person.

As Tony Robbins says, "If you're not progressing, you're dying."

Life is all about progress, and progress equals happiness in whatever area we choose it to be. Work, hobbies, relationships… the list goes on.

This is why I feel I have to get this message out loud and proud. Work on yourself. Work on yourself some more. If you fuck up, learn from your mistakes and then work on yourself some more. For me, having suffered my problems relating to my career, I follow the motto to:

> "Work harder on yourself than you do on your job."
> Jim Rohn

It is my job to work on my self-development. I am my very own project! This book was my counsellor.

You can be your own project too! You must be your own project!

I realise that this isn't probably the warmest introduction to me; some of you may be able to relate and some not. (Some may think, **Wow this lad can whinge…** and whinge I did!). However, behind the brave face and confident personality, it shaped my wellbeing for a long period and I feel it needed to be highlighted. I am on a much healthier path now, with a much higher appreciation for life. I still have some challenging days (we all do and will always continue to do so), but I also have learned to appreciate how fortunate I am to be here. I want to make sure that the time I do have on this planet is as enjoyable as it possibly can be for me, but also for others. Seriously, we get one chance at this; happiness is so important. I want to live life on my terms now and I am very much determined to do that, as well as making others feel better on the way.

From the negative experiences, a more positive approach to life has been formed. This can happen to anybody.

WHAT I SEE AS PERSONAL GROWTH
self-help, self-development and other terminology

So thus far, you have an introduction into my background and it gives you an indication of some of the issues that were holding me back. However, this book is about you.

If you have ever suffered from any of the above feelings, then I hope this book can help you as I begin to give some tips that you can start implementing to help live a more fulfilled life. If your already involved in this, I hope it really hammers home the message to keep on improving.

Looking through just some of the terminology, some of the definitions include:
- Personal growth – the ongoing process of understanding and developing oneself in order to achieve one's fullest potential.
- Self-help – designed to assist people in achieving things for themselves.

- Self-development – taking steps to better yourself, such as by learning new skills or overcoming bad habits.

It all covers anything that deals with helping or improving you. I used it to develop my overall mental wellbeing, and therefore, it is a life skill that must be developed daily. To me, it is literally the most important area of your life. You may see it reflected in this book under different terminology, but the overall meaning for me is always the same… as is my message… to keep improving or to strive to better yourself. I honestly believe it is the secret to a good life. So although I said there wasn't a 'magic' formula, there isn't, but self-improvement does help.

I also must stress again that you don't have to be suffering from poor wellbeing to engage in self-development; it just turns out I was when I began.

For anybody already involved in self-development, you will have likely seen/heard a number of these suggestions before; as stated, I am not reinventing the wheel here. However, there is obviously a reason we consistently see these things coming up in books; they can help. To really gain maximum benefits from them, we must consistently work with them and it must become a lifestyle habit. How I see it is, engaging in positive material daily should be as habitual as brushing your teeth, it is that important!

For anybody new to this field, try to start implementing the following tips and see if it has a positive influence. I would be extremely shocked if you see no changes at all in how you felt day to day. For anyone already involved in self-development, I hope I can enlighten you with some of the Joe Bloggs approach.

GUIDANCE ON 'FINDING YOURSELF'

If, perhaps, you're feeling a little lost in life or you wish to understand why you do what you do. Or you simply need a little bit of motivation.

FEELING STUCK ISN'T NECESSARILY A BAD THING

> *"If you feel stuck, do what you can until you find clarity, but don't stop moving forward. Action creates breakthroughs."*
> Wendy Nicole Anderson

I want to talk about the notion of 'feeling stuck'. The reason being that when I was really struggling, this was the expression or feeling I kept referring to. This phrase just seemed to 'plague' my thoughts.

How I referred to it was in relation to the emptiness I felt, and mine always stemmed from 'feeling stuck' at work or with a career and almost 'feeling lost' in life. For me, it has taken some real soul-searching.

Some of you may have experienced feeling stuck in different ways. Some of you may never have experienced it.

For me, it was a constant feeling of not knowing what I wanted to do as a career or feeling trapped in my job... Who did I want to be? What did I want to do? I just 'felt stuck' in life.

A lot of people around me seemed to have their lives worked out; their career was set. I had worked in several different sectors (which I felt was frowned upon – even though, to be fair, I did fairly well in a lot of them) and I had finished university. I was hard-working, but I felt like I was supposed to have everything worked out, but I didn't (although I now recognise this is not the case), and as a result, it dragged me down.

I came across something by a renowned speaker, Mel Robbins, that really changed my thoughts on this. She says that 'feeling stuck' is not a bad thing. She says it is the way you think about the experience of being stuck. Feeling stuck is just a signal from our body. Just like when our body is hungry and sends us signals that we need to eat and feeling tired is a fundamental sign that we need to sleep. Feeling stuck works in the same way. It is a signal from our heart and soul that we need personal growth.

Personal growth is one of the most fundamental needs of all human beings. This is why I have become fucking obsessed with it, and ironically, I am a lot happier now too.

When we have stopped growing in life, our job, relationships, etc., we can start to feel stuck.

However, unfortunately, most of us make the mistake of thinking about how stuck we feel and get trapped into bad thinking patterns in our heads (this was me!).

But this is the last thing we should be doing. It should be a sign that action needs to be taken. So now, it is about finding deliberate ways to do just this.

This can be related to any part of your life.

If you're 'stuck' in work, perhaps it's time for a change – you need to develop your skills or engage in a new project. You may need a new job altogether.

If you're in a relationship and you feel stuck, perhaps it's about trying to invest some more time and spark things up a little. Or perhaps it has run its course.

Perhaps you are a sportsman who is seeing a lack of results, and perhaps you need to seek out new training methods.

Perhaps you feel stuck, and you don't know who you truly want to be (this is what I was always feeling like); in this case, it's time to do some soul-searching.

The point being, if you are feeling 'stuck' and you feel like you're not moving forward, try to understand that this is your mind and body trying to give you a message. Perhaps widen your knowledge in a specific area or seek new opportunities and see if this has a positive impact. Most importantly, start taking some action.

I still get these feelings sometimes... they will creep up. However, I never ever stop trying to better myself on a personal level. I want you to have the same attitude to your life.

Journal

If there is an area in life you feel you are struggling in, write it in the area below and give yourself some ideas to approach it differently. Start listing ideas to help you move forward using the probing questions as help.

Probing Questions:

- Is there something I can try outside my comfort zone?
- Is there something I can change/can I try something different?
- How could I make this more fun?
- What is the opposite of my current approach?
- Could I reach out to someone/something for additional support?
- What is standing in my way? Is there a solution to this problem?
- What tools do I need to move forwards?
- What could I do right now that I have been avoiding?
- What do I want the most right now?

FEELING STUCK ISN'T NECESSARILY A BAD THING

Also use this area to add any extra notes you may have from the section above.

TRY TO FIND YOUR 'WHY'

"When you know your why, you will know your way."
Michael Hyatt

I feel another massive tip to help you prosper is to find out what your 'why' is. Now here I pay tribute to some important advice which I have learned. It's something I try to apply to my every day to help me gain fulfilment in life and really understand 'why' I am doing the things I do.

Simon Sinek, who is a very influential entrepreneur, has written several fantastic books such as *Start with Why* and *Find Your Why*. He believes your 'why' is about having a higher purpose in life than simply looking to make money. He claims that if you can 'find your why', anything is achievable, and life feels more fulfilling.

I use this as a sense of motivation but also as a cross-check to make sure what I am doing is worthwhile (I still get it wrong sometimes too). It is a good way to check whether you are investing your time correctly. It's the internal engine inside that says this is why I'm doing it; it can be the driving force behind everything.

'Why' I work on my personal development is because I recognise I have further potential, and it positively serves me. 'Why' I want to write this book is to spread these positive messages, and I don't want others to feel the way I felt.

I hope to inspire other people! I want people to see that they should be grateful for life, for people to see that we can shift our thought process. If people want to become a better version of themselves, I want them to be inspired to do so. I want to give people tools to help them feel better. It sounds a little 'out there', but I now feel like I want to leave something a little more lasting in the world.

This 'why', for me, is enough to motivate me to keep going forward, and this personal journey is giving me purpose each day. It is giving me purpose to keep on writing, to keep posting and to keep growing.

You can instantly see the driving force that is connected here. I have a big 'why' and it serves me positively. However, this book is not about me; it is about you. So, I want *you* to understand your 'why'.

Your 'why'

Why is it that you do what you do? It may be that this section is about finding deeper purpose and therefore has some thought-provoking questions. It may be that you need a little reminder about why you do what you currently do in work, or a reminder of your business's purpose, but I want you to give it some consideration.

Dean Graziosi, in his book *Millionaire Success Habits*, suggests a technique labelled '7 levels deep' as a process for self-discovery. It can be carried out with a partner and involves asking the 'why' question seven times.

The answer you give forms the basis for the next question and it is designed to go deeper into your motivations. For example, you might say that starting your own business is the most important thing to you in life, and then you would ask 'why' this is; it could be to spend more time with your family – again, 'why' is this important? You ask this 'why' question seven times to really uncover your motives.

This is just a hypothetical example, but you can use this process yourself. You need to remember your 'why', because it is going to help you on the days that you feel like giving up, or you lack motivation.

Included below is blank space to allow you to journal and to probe deeper. List in the space your hobby. Or put in your job. Or your business. Or put in your dream job and why this would serve you. Put anything you want in. Your family and why this is so important to you. Put in anything that you feel is important to you. Then ask yourself some probing questions and answer them around the topic. Make notes. Scribble away.

Probing questions:

- What is most important to you in life? Why is it important? Why do you love doing it?
- What is your definition of success? Why is it that? Why do you get out of bed in the morning?

TRY TO FIND YOUR 'WHY'

Hopefully by viewing your 'why', it will give you some insight. If you are currently working on a project and finding yourself becoming disengaged, then use this as a reminder to motivate you.

If you are doing well already, but you know there is room for growth, reflect on your why and use it to push you even further forward.

If your 'why' is not aligned with what you are doing now, then perhaps it's time to look for a change.

If you truly can't find your 'why' and you feel unfulfilled, perhaps you're doing the wrong thing, and it's time to search out alternative answers.

I do not want to tell you what to do with your life here; I simply want you to gain an understanding for yourself.

Also remember your 'why' can change at different moments throughout life, and if this is the case, this is OK. However, by using this process as a guideline and a reflective tool, we can ensure we are on the right track and keep motivated at all times.

If you have scribbled it in your journal and it's positive and uplifting, write it on another big piece of paper and stick it in the middle of your wall and remind yourself every single fucking day why you're doing what you do! This stuff is powerful and yet it is so simple.

THE ART OF FULFILMENT

> "Success without fulfilment
> is the ultimate failure."
> Tony Robbins

I think closely correlated to the above is what Tony Robbins calls 'the art of fulfilment'. For me, it is so important because I often described myself as feeling 'empty' or 'unfulfilled'. He describes this as one of two pillars that are needed to create an 'extraordinary life'. He believes 'fulfilment' is art because, for every single person, it is different. For what might be beautiful to one person could be ugly to the next. What lights us up is completely different. He explains that what makes us feel fulfilled on the inside is about having a life of meaning. It correlates very strongly with having a 'purpose' or 'finding your why'. He believes it is critical that we find out what this is, because when you are fulfilled, you are more inclined to achieve more.

I feel the reason I was so unhappy with a lot of things I was doing was because I knew I wanted something different. However, all these questions were having a serious impact on my welfare. I certainly didn't want to settle with being miserable. I don't want anyone to settle with being miserable.

Again, if you are left feeling unfulfilled at present, perhaps it is time to question what you are doing in your life. It doesn't have to be career-related; it could be related to any aspect of your life. Our lives are too short to be anything but happy.

Tony explains that we should always find our 'pull' when it comes to whatever it is you are trying to achieve. The reason being is that pushing for something requires willpower. However, when you are 'pulled' towards something, something so exciting or so attractive or what you desire so much, it becomes so much more motivating. It makes you want to get out of bed in the morning; it makes you want to work on it till late in the evening. For me, it is this book and my desire to get it finished. It is also the Joe Bloggs Talks brand to spread my messages of positivity and inspire people. This gives me real genuine motivation.

What is it for you? Again, if you have something you really want to achieve, then put it down here. Keep reminding yourself of this.

You may already be doing something you absolutely love; if this is the case, then great – just keep reminding yourself.

Push and pull

- What would get me out of bed in the morning with a pure sense of joy and fulfilment?
- Is what I am doing now making me truly happy? Or am I forcing myself to engage in certain areas of my life?
- What would be my dream occupation?

- If money was no object, what would I want to do with my life?
- What is it that I love about what I do currently?
- What have I always wanted to do but I have let self-doubt or fear stand in the way?

Anything that gets you thinking about what motivates you.

Also use this area to add any extra notes you may have from the section above.

GUIDANCE TO GAIN SOME CONTROL OF YOUR LIFE

If you find yourself easily influenced by others. You struggle with the opinions of other people. You blame everything else for any problems. Or you constantly wish you had other people's lives.

LEARN TO LET GO OF THE OPINIONS OF OTHERS

Another way for me to live a fuller life, and to start developing personally, was to start letting go of the opinions of other people. This section is quite in depth as I was personally terrible with it.

> "No one can make you feel inferior without your consent."
> Eleanor Roosevelt

This is career-related again, but being only twenty-nine and working in a variety of roles, I previously gained some interesting opinions from other people:

"You're at university, and you're working behind a bar... what ambition have you got?"

"You're studying a Mickey Mouse degree in Sports Science... what a waste of time... you should do something real like engineering."

> *"You're changing jobs again… you need to grow up and settle down."*
>
> *"You can never stick anything out."*
>
> *"You're doing this job now… when are you going to get a real job?"* The worst one!

These are just to name a few; I could literally write a book on the opinions of other people, and I believe we all could.

Now I am not solely blaming other people's opinions for my depression, but it had an impact on me as I was already battling with my thoughts and this was adding fuel to the fire.

Perhaps, reflecting, there was some weakness in my character. I now know that I can choose the way that I react to people's opinions of me. We all can! And as I worked on myself, I have also now come to realise that other people's opinions should mean absolutely fuck all when it comes to choosing what you want to do with your life. This is huge progress.

Now, this is not easy because as human beings, we often seek approval. As children, we look for approval from our parents for the things we say and behaviour we carry out. Then as we get older, we often do the same with our peers; it gives us a sense of comfort or validation.

As well as this, if we think about receiving criticism (which is someone else's opinion), this can be used in a positive sense if given constructively. I will take this all day long. I will even take some harsh truths and criticisms if given to assist me and my development. I have played sport from a young age; it isn't that I must be wrapped in cotton wool. What I mean here is, if someone is trying to drag you down, belittle you, mock you or in any way chip in with their fucking ten pence worth about what you should be doing or how you should be living your life... well, you have to learn to let go of this and do what is best for you.

I have some friends who have said they don't let the opinions of others bother them, and I had always questioned how true this was (because I felt I took it so personally). I would often think it was bravado; however, I have now realised that it is possible to get to this state of mind, but I think it does take practise.

We ultimately must realise that we are under no compulsion to live up to the expectations of other people and in doing so, we are just wasting our energy on other people. If this is what guides you and you make all your decisions based on what other people might think, then it will become so mentally draining, you have to be prepared to upset people and to do the things that you want to do. It may involve upsetting a few people on the way, but ultimately it will serve you much more in your future.

Regarding other people's opinions, try not to let them completely guide you as well. You may have something deep inside you that you want to achieve, but you may have other people who are trying to push you away from it (I emphasise push — because we need to let our pull be stronger — consider the Tony Robbins theory discussed previously again). We have to realise that sometimes this may come from a place of love, for example, a family member may point you in a direction that they think is best for you (such as going to college or university — like my parents, who tied together my obvious affection for sport as a kid), so in their hearts, they think they are doing things in your best interest. In addition to this, they might tell you not to go ahead with something because they are trying to protect you. If you are thinking of leaving your job and starting a business, they may try to stop you because they think you are making a bad decision and you should stay 'safe' and keep your job to pay your bills. They don't want to see you get hurt or they think you're making a decision that is not in your best interest. However, to put this simply… this is your life, nobody else's. It just so happens that I didn't know who the fuck I wanted to be.

But let me just make this clear again, so it really sinks in: do not let the opinion of *other people* dictate how *you* feel!

Your happiness is your choice.

Now I am not so naive to think that I am the only person who has ever done this. We will all have done it in some way or another, and it is not always related to your career choice:

"I daren't go out in that dress… what if X says something about it?"

"I can't go for dinner with X group as it might upset X group."

"I really want to go for that job, but my family don't think it's good for me, so I am not going to."

This literally happens to so many of us every single day!

Do not let it be you! Be a little bit selfish. If you really want to do something, but at the expense of perhaps upsetting others, be brave to say no. Be polite about it, but remember it's your life and nobody else's.

What was worst of all, I would often find myself trying

to justify myself to others. In relation to the bar work, people would often say things to demoralise my work. I remember seeing one of my former teachers from junior school (as if he remembered me!) and they made a demoralising comment about working in a bar. I responded, "Ohhh, it's just temporary while I'm at university," but ultimately, it was just adding to my feeling of failure and I was trying to sell myself short. However, the truth is, why did it even matter? Because I wasn't in a high-paying corporate job, I was made to feel little? It really used to fucking wind me up. More importantly, who the fucking hell are you to tell me what I should be doing with my life?

It is such an ugly trait of society.

The late Heath Ledger once said:

> "Everyone you ever meet always asks if you have a career, are married or own a house, as if life is some kind of grocery list, but nobody ever asks if you if you are happy."

Perhaps, if we just stopped for a minute to ask someone we loved if they were happy, like truly happy, and stopped judging people based on such things, we would have less problems.

However, it is something that will continue to prevail; it is just about how we choose to react to it, and this is the key to our development. As you can see from the unpolite vocabulary here, it wound me up, but I used to hold on to it then, it wasn't until I starting learning to let go, until I chose to not react in such a way that I could begin to free myself from it. I was so hostile.

Once again: if you are happy in what you are doing, then stop justifying your actions to other people.

It does not matter what area of life this refers to. The truth is, everyone is entitled to an opinion, so let them have it, try not to dwell on it, certainly don't let it hold you back.

If I tell some certain people I am hoping to release a book one day, I am sure they will have an opinion, but I cannot let this stop me. The old me would have allowed this to influence me; I would never have even tried it, which is sad but true.

That said, I am not saying that I am made of steel now and I *never* get affected by this. Sometimes I do still find myself affected by the opinions of others (more so those who are closest to me) as I am only human.

In addition to this, if I received a number of rubbish reviews for this book, it would probably hurt slightly (so be kind, ha-ha), but I certainly can't let it stop me trying.

For me this concept of other people's opinions is definitely less prominent than it used to be, and it is truly life-changing. It takes practise, but you begin to get more emotional intelligence, and I am slowly teaching myself to not even rise to this in whatever area of life it is that someone may try to bring me down in. I must try and not become too angry or upset or depressed by somebody else's opinion. It is just not worth my energy. It is giving them power over me, and I refuse to allow that to happen. People can say what they want to me; however, it is down to me how I choose to react and this is what we should all focus on. This is what I want you to take from this. I use my examples as I want them to help you.

It may be that people's comments motivate you and that

is great; this is a much healthier response than sitting and dwelling on it and letting it create a negative mood.

However, if you let other people's opinions guide you or affect your mood, then you are allowing people power over you. In order to regain your power and have full control over your life, you must realise that you are in the driving seat. It is you who can prevent this.

If someone is to give a constructive opinion with feedback and guidance, then listen (it helps your personal growth); however, if someone wants to be a dickhead for the sake of it, and it's going to stop you doing what you want to do in your life, then you need to let that go.

BE THE CHANGE IN YOUR LIFE

Change only happens when you take full responsibility for *your* life

> "When you stop blaming others for your suffering and take responsibility for your own happiness, you shift from a place of victimhood to a place of power."
>
> Unknown

> "No one is responsible for your happiness but yourself."
>
> Will Smith

Too often, we play the victim. I did it myself; I would blame my parents for certain aspects of my life, or I would blame other people around me for making me feel inferior, as explained. I would often be looking for an excuse to blame someone else for the way I felt. In my angry rage of bitterness, I would even blame the university system for 'making me choose a shit degree' or not 'giving me the correct advice' – how barmy is that!

Do not get me wrong, there were incidents where people's words or actions did hurt me, and in some circumstances, the other person was at fault, and there will be incidents in the future of my life where I will suffer hurt and pain from others, but it is up to me to choose how I react to these.

These were genuinely only minor incidents and I appreciate that people have suffered some truly horrific life events that have had major impacts on their lives.

However, positive change only happens when you take full responsibility for your life. Nobody will do it for you.

There are people who have suffered extremely horrific upbringings and still went on to live extremely fulfilling lives.

They are in absolutely no way responsible for what happened to them, but they have chosen how they have reacted. I doubt these people spent their lives dwelling on the fact that they chose the wrong university course; this is minor shit in comparison.

There is something referred to as 'post-traumatic growth'. This refers to a positive personality change following traumatic life events. Experiencing a traumatic event can have a transforming role in some personalities, which can facilitate growth. I know my circumstances are hardly traumatic to most, but I like to believe I am using it to channel it in a more positive way now.

It is up to you to control your own destiny. If you are not where you want to be in life right now, start making actions and goals on how you're going to get there. Then work on becoming one per cent better each day to try and reach your goal.

However, stop looking for excuses and blaming other people for the choices you have made.

> *"The sooner you change, the sooner your future will."*
> Steven Green

In addition to this, your thoughts will try and tell you every reason why you should not be doing something. The inner critic will start telling you why it can't be done. It will tell you every single excuse about why you should stop. It is up to you to take back control.

Take back control

Here is a basic exercise to try and help us move forward with something we feel we are currently held back by. This could be our thoughts, beliefs or even excuses we are telling ourselves. It could be related to any aspect of your life.

The number one area in my life I am going to take control of is:

_____
_____
_____
_____
_____
_____

I am going to stop using the excuses of:

_____
_____
_____

_____
_____
_____
_____

The first action I am going to take with this is:

_____
_____
_____
_____
_____
_____
_____

You may scribble other keynotes, which will help you take action on this now.

_____
_____
_____
_____
_____
_____
_____

Also use this area to add any extra notes you may have from the section above.

EVERYTHING COMES DOWN TO DECISIONS

Really understand how decisions can influence our lives

As I was listening to two of my favourite speakers, Les Brown and Tony Robbins, they talked about the importance of decisions.

Decisions = our destiny.

Think about your life and think of some of the decisions you have made; had you made a different decision, the outcome would have been completely different.

We tend to sway towards negative, so try to think of the positive examples too.

What we choose to eat each day and whether we choose to exercise or not influences our physical destiny. Likewise, what we decide to focus our thoughts on can influence our mental state of mind.

We have decisions and choices which only we can make. If we want a new life or experience, then we must take control and make a decision to change it.

If you don't like your job, you can change it. If you don't like what you are eating for your body, you can change it. If you don't like your relationship, you can change it. Whatever area it is – yes, you can change it.

If you want to change your results, you have to become more conscious in your decision-making. Make wiser decisions and take action to achieve things.

I know what you're thinking – is this a realistic approach to life? The job you hate pays the bills, whereas following your passion is risky and potentially unsafe. I get that.

If it is a decision that involves making a serious change, then it's perhaps best speaking with loved ones first, making plans, strategies, etc. if that makes you feel more at ease. However, the fundamental truth is that if you wanted to change something, you can do it at any moment you wish. That's the truth. Too many of us settle on the excuses that we tell ourselves; this is because it keeps things 'easy' or avoids us having to do something uncomfortable. Believe me, I have done it myself on many occasions.

However, if there is something you are thinking about doing, then at the very least, just start making those decisions and act on them. This is something you can do! I am not telling you to leave your job now and forget about your bills, or to suddenly start running a marathon if you never engage in fitness. However, you can do something today. Taking action is key.

I love the following quote, although I don't know the origin:

> "Start by doing one push up. Start by drinking one cup of water. Start by paying towards one debt. Start by reading one page. Start by making one sale. Start by deleting one old contact. Start by walking one lap. Start by attending one event. Start today. Repeat tomorrow."
>
> Unknown

All we must do is start. For me, in this instance, it started with a journal, which then lead to a sentence, to a paragraph, to a chapter, to moving on to a book. However, it had to start somewhere. It can be the same for you. If you have a vision or a dream that you know you really want to pursue, then start pursuing it. If you do want to lose weight, then start with a short walk. Do anything, just make sure you make the decision to start.

If you are not happy with what you are doing, but you don't yet know what you want to do, start exploring what makes you happy. Start investing some time in yourself.

STOP COMPARING YOURSELF TO OTHERS

> "Every minute you spend wishing you had someone else's life is a minute spent wasting yours."
>
> Unknown

> "Comparison is an act of violence against the self."
>
> Iyanla Vanzan

I touched on it briefly earlier: a lot of my unhappiness stemmed from not seeing myself as successful in comparison to my friends and only viewing earning lots of money as the 'pinnacle of success'.

However, as proven, this does not automatically result in happiness. It certainly wasn't helping me feel happy.

Now, this isn't saying, do not have role models or people you wish to aspire to be – this can be healthy if managed correctly. However, we must try our best to stop comparing ourselves to others if this is in a negative sense, and we must recognise we are truly our own individual person.

When it comes to comparing ourselves to others, we can do this in countless ways. Relationships, careers, physical shape, physical looks or material wealth – the list is endless. However, it serves no purpose other than to make us feel like shit. Yet despite this, so many of us constantly do it.

We live in a world now where social media constantly surrounds us, and our day-to-day lives can be spent looking at other people's 'picture perfect' lifestyles. *The Subtle Art of Not Giving a F*ck* book by Mark Manson says measuring your worth by comparing yourself to others will only lead to disappointment and this is a shitty value that can derail your path to happiness. It is so true!

Manson also says using your material success as a yardstick for life is another shitty value. It is a common trap we fall into – wanting a bigger car or nicer house than our neighbours (sometimes referred to as 'keeping up with the Joneses') – but this doesn't lead to better wellbeing. He points to studies that show that once our basic needs are cared for, extra wealth doesn't increase happiness, and chasing wealth can have a detrimental effect on our health if we choose to pursue it over family, honesty and integrity.

Therefore, there ultimately needs to be a balance, and if you are chasing only money and wealth, then do so with a healthy intention.

Jim Carey once said:

> "I think everyone should get rich and famous and do everything they ever dreamed of so that they can see it is not the answer."

This is a pretty bold statement given that most of us often dream of getting rich. I have it in my goals to earn more financially. I still know more money would make my life 'easier' in terms of giving me more freedom, and I would enjoy having more money. I am not denying that. Also I am not going to lecture you on how money doesn't make you happy; that's none of my business because it may just do that for you.

However, we often hear of tragic tales of people seen to 'have it all' yet still suffering from issues such as depression (many because they're not fulfilled), some even tragically taking their own lives. It's genuinely fucking heart-breaking. So, whilst you should have ambition and be driven (I do not deny this because I think it's an admirable trait), you need to learn to be happy in this very moment and grateful for what you do have now. I can't stress this enough. I know this sounds fucking tragic and quite cliché, but we could literally die tomorrow – do you want to die miserable or do you want to try and make each day as happy as you possibly can? If you spend your whole time wishing you were somebody else and comparing your life to someone else's, then how will you ever be truly happy? Nothing would ever be enough. This is, again, why self-development was so important to me because it taught me these principles.

Instead of comparing yourself, find a role model or a mentor and engage in self-competition

If you are inspired by somebody you know rather than looking at them in a jealous sense or comparing yourself to them, speak with them and learn from them; use it in a positive sense. More people will be prepared to help you than you think. Get a mentor, someone who can lead you to where you want to be.

In addition to this, engage in self-competition. In the book *Life's Amazing Secrets* by Gaur Gopal Das, the principle of self-competition is highlighted: rather than always competing with others, their possessions or power or privilege, you should do so with yourself instead.

He highlights actor Matthew McConaughey, who, in an Oscar-acceptance speech back in 2014, demonstrated this very trait.

As he told it, McConaughey, at age fifteen, was asked who his hero was. After some reflection, he replied, "It's me in ten years." A decade later, the same person asked him if he'd become a hero. The twenty-five-year-old McConaughey replied, "Not even close – because my hero's me at thirty-five."

This is inspiring and something we can learn from. All you can do is your best each day. In Japanese culture, there is something called '*kaizen*', which means never-ending improvement. We can always push to be better, and this can be in business, life or any area. By adopting this attitude, you are setting yourself up to live a more prosperous and fulfilled life.

Competing with yourself rather than others will inspire you to always do your best, on your terms, and thus help you achieve your full potential. I have become engrossed in this 'self-improvement' philosophy to life.

GUIDANCE SURROUNDING YOUR THOUGHTS

If you constantly doubt yourself, give yourself a hard time mentally or you want to learn ways to boost your positivity.

DIRECTING YOUR THOUGHTS MORE POSITIVELY
– 'switching gears'

> "Positive thinking will let you do everything better than negative thinking will."
>
> Zig Ziglar

I agree that in certain situations, it can feel challenging to 'just think more positively'. There have been occasions in my own life where I have felt that no amount of optimistic thinking was going to help me and if someone had told me to 'stay positive', I would have lost my shit. There are occasions where you need to be just allowed to feel the way that you do. You need to process these thoughts and emotions. Even as someone who believes so strongly in these concepts, I still understand that shit happens.

Your partner just left you and you lost your job on the

same day: "Ah, OK, well, try to think positively." ...fuck off!

I want to express that I am a real person and I don't walk around in protective positive bubble wrap. I stress this in all the content I talk about.

However, with that said, there is no denying that having a more positive outlook in any situation is going to make you feel better about it. No matter what that is.

In regards to working on my issues (mine being hugely connected with career choices, as you probably gathered), I realised that in order to move forward, I had to get rid of my own negative beliefs and thoughts, which I felt were stopping me from moving forward.

So how did I do this? First I realised that the decisions I had made in the past could not be changed.

I also learned to channel my negative thoughts and beliefs differently. So when the negative ruminations started, I could change the thoughts I was having. I heard this once referred to as 'switching gears'.

So now, I try to look at everything I have done in life thus far as either a positive or a learning curve.

So as an example, let's visit some of my past choices.

Thought/area	Previous negative thought	More positive thought
My degree was a waste of five years.	I will never get that time back – how stupid, I should never have gone in the first place.	I would have perhaps done things differently, but I can't change the past! I learned a lot of great skills, which I still utilise to this day!

Not continuing with a previous business idea.	Here I go again, getting sick of something. I can't stick anything out; I'm a complete failure! Everyone I told will think I am an idiot.	I put a lot of effort in, but it wasn't really a passion; I learned skills and was put out of my comfort zone on several occasions, which will be great for my development.
I still don't know what I want to do in life.	I will never ever find happiness; I will always be in this situation.	Keep working on myself; good things will come.

As you can see, I changed my thoughts to view things differently. I now see my past experiences as all part of my journey so far. Therefore, even though I have not got to where I want to be just yet, I believe all my experience will serve to help me achieve this going forward. I now feel like I am definitely heading the right way.

Now, this isn't saying I don't sometimes revert to negative thoughts because I sometimes do – we are only human, after all – but it's about continuously working on reprogramming those thoughts to be positive and not allowing them to drag me down. The reason being that this will serve you nothing. I cannot stress enough that you should keep a close eye on the stories you are telling yourself. It can literally be the difference between feeling great and in control or feeling like shit and completely helpless.

It's also important to recognise the *past* is the *past*, and we can't change it; we can only focus on what we can change moving forward. If we keep referring to 'what if' questions or reflecting on what can't be changed, we can never progress in life.

Journal

I now want you to try something similar now: write down any thoughts you have, or stories that you currently tell yourself which are negative or harmful, and I want you to reprogram them to change them to give yourself a more positive outlook.

Take however long you need on this exercise. Becoming more aware of our negative thoughts is the first step to self-awareness.

Previous negative thought →	New positive thought

If you are still struggling to do this and we are still drawn to any experience as negative, try to use a negative experience as motivation to make a positive change; everything that we do in life or choose to do is an opportunity for personal growth.

Perhaps jot down a negative experience and think about how you are going to use that in a positive sense going forward.

As well as this, you may not be able to think of any current negative thoughts you have. However, moving forwards, keep this exercise in mind, and next time you become aware of such thoughts, try to think of alternative positive replacement thoughts, as these are going to serve you better.

Also use this area to add any extra notes you may have from the section above.

CREATING POSITIVE THOUGHTS

Why we need positive thoughts

> "Keep your thoughts positive because your thoughts become your words. Keep your words positive because your words become your behaviour. Keep your behaviour positive because your behaviour becomes your habits. Keep your habits positive because your habits become your values. Keep your values positive because your values become your destiny."
>
> Ghandi

Experts estimate that the mind thinks between sixty to eighty thousand thoughts a day. That's an average of 2,500–3,300 thoughts per hour. That's incredible. Other experts estimate a smaller number of fifty thousand thoughts per day, which means about 2,100 thoughts per hour.

That's a hell of a lot of thoughts, isn't it? Everything starts with thought, so be wise and careful what you think about. Training our mental health is just as important, if not more important, than our physical health.

Jim Rohn refers to our 'mental factory' or our 'mental toolbox' which we pour thoughts into every single day. We need to fill it with positivity.

If we fill our bodies with rubbish foods such as fizzy drinks, crisps, chocolate and snacks, we become overweight, we suffer health problems and we can become sick.

If we fill our head with rubbish thoughts and negativity, we become sick – so we must try to avoid this.

As Jim states, in order to build the right life, we must select the right tools and keep out the wrong ones. Therefore, we must fill it with positive materials, books and knowledge, as well as positive people.

Our mind is literally our strongest asset, and you are 'sitting at the controls'. You are in charge. Make it as positive as you can each day.

USE POSITIVE LANGUAGE AND SELF-TALK

> "Self-talk is the most powerful form of communication because it either empowers you or it defeats you."
>
> Unknown

Your quality of life can be determined by the communication you have with yourself.

You therefore need to become conscious of the words you speak to yourself. I have been there. "I am a fucking failure." "I will never amount to anything." I have said these out loud, and I have repeatedly thought them inside my head. This can absolutely crucify you. If you start believing such things, it is going to make change so much more difficult.

Jim Kwik explains that we must be 'killing ANTS' (automatic negative thoughts). He claims our brain is like a supercomputer and your self-talk will help it run. So, program it well. Our mind is eavesdropping on our self-talk, and if we fight for our limitations, we get to keep them (meaning if we keep telling ourselves, **I am not good enough**, we will begin to take this as truth and our life decisions will be made with this in our minds).

There is a metaphor related to the awful conditioning of elephants with sticks. Elephants are often used as tourist attractions in certain parts of the world. Elephant handlers use only small ropes tied to the ground with tiny sticks to keep an elephant in place. The reason it works is because when they are younger, the handlers tie the elephants to huge trunks with large ropes. The young elephants pull and tug and fight until they tire themselves out, and they soon learn that they cannot move when tied up. The handlers use increasingly smaller ropes and sticks, but the elephants never tug them and they have learned that they simply cannot move when tied up.

One of the largest and strongest animals in the world limited by something a child could escape from.

We can relate that to us as humans and self-talk. Think about the limitations we can set for ourselves. If we believe we can never do it or won't ever achieve it and we consistently tell ourselves daily we can't, then we will start to believe this. As a result, we will not take the action required to achieve something because we have defeated ourselves before we have begun. As human beings, we act and follow up on who we believe we are, and we act consistently with it. Therefore, as a lesson, become very conscious of the words you say to yourself, ensuring they are positive.

As one of my favourite coaches, Paul Mort, says, "Mind your fucking language," and it's referring to the language we say to ourselves.

Try a morning of listening to positive affirmations (section to follow) and start your day right.

I once heard at a seminar that the two most essential words in the English language are 'I am', which stems from having belief in you.

There is a big difference between telling yourself daily that 'I am capable' compared to 'I am a failure'. Yet I consistently told myself the latter; it is little wonder I felt like shit! Use your self-talk to your advantage!

POSITIVE AFFIRMATIONS

Positive affirmations can help you to challenge and overcome negative thoughts. When you repeat them, start to believe in them, you can begin to make positive changes.

Positive affirmations should be catered to you; they can be used to override those negative belief patterns. As a starting principle, I will show you some of the affirmations I have used to overcome my toxic thoughts:

I am entitled to happiness.
I am capable of change.
I am successful.

Positive affirmations can be used in the morning as part of a routine to help boost positive feelings. They can be used when 'psyching yourself up' for something, perhaps a talk at work or prior to a sporting competition. Make them unique to you, but use them to ensure you don't fall victim to self-sabotaging thoughts.

Remember Muhammad Ali?! "I am the greatest." He said

this to himself even before he was recognised in the world as the greatest; he believed in himself so strongly. To some, it may have been arrogance, but to him, it was an unshakeable self-belief in himself.

The principle is often to say them out loud to yourself; however, you might feel fucking stupid doing it that way – I get it. I do, I won't lie. I will often play audiotapes in the car with just a reel of positive affirmations, letting myself listen to the positive wording going in. I find this is great first thing in the morning to start the day right, but it can be used at any time. I will sometimes say them quietly to myself if I feel negative thought patterns creeping in (the narrator in your head). Find out what works for you. I have been at seminars literally screaming this stuff at the top of my voice before; I will be honest… It didn't feel like me, and I wanted the ground to just swallow me up. I have adapted it to work for me and you can do the same. You could start with something simple, such as getting your notebook (journal) and writing some sentences in there which are going to help motivate you or serve you positively.

STOP WITH NEGATIVE RUMINATIONS

In addition to some of the points made above, negative ruminations emotionally hijack us and strengthen our negative feelings. They rarely offer new insights or explanations on how to handle situations and, therefore, essentially make us prisoners in our own thoughts. A dangerous place to be.

It is the flip side to positive self-talk. Constant ruminations can make you more likely to experience depression or anxiety. This was me.

If you spend a lot of time ruminating, it can lead to a snowball effect. Once you get into a ruminating thought cycle, it can be hard to get out of it. If you do start having such thoughts, it is important to stop them as quickly as possible to prevent them from becoming more intense.

Think of a ball rolling downhill; it's easier to stop the ruminating thoughts when they start rolling and have less speed than when they have gathered momentum.

I also once heard at a seminar about a 'finger in the fire'

analogy. The idea is that if we simply touched a burning fire with our fingertip, we would be left with a bit of discomfort. However, if we were to keep our finger in the fire for a long period, we would start to get some significant pain and long-term damage.

The same principle refers to our thoughts. If we have one or two negative thoughts regarding a scenario, whilst it can be discomforting and cause us pain, we, to some extent, can break the cycle quickly and change our pattern of thought. However, the longer we spend in those thoughts, the more chance they have of developing into regular patterns of negative thoughts, the pain worsens and it becomes severely discomforting.

It is something I suffered significantly with. What started as a thought surrounding a bad career choice would end in me thinking my whole life was worthless when in reality, this couldn't be further from the truth.

I used to get 'stuck' in these thoughts regularly for weeks and months, unable to shift them. Now, if I ever feel them coming on, or hearing myself saying them, I knowingly try to break them quickly. I try to get my finger out the fucking fire before it starts to have a serious burden on my welfare.

Many will have been victim to this at some point. Here is a generic example to illustrate the point:

> "I look so stupid in this outfit. No wonder I can't get a date. Why can't I lose weight? It's impossible; I'm going to be on my own forever."

This is just one example off the top of my head. However, a lot of us do this to ourselves in our own individual way.

Do you do this? If so, give yourself a fucking break. Stop the self-sabotaging. Or, use it as motivation. I am going to make positive changes. I am going to be healthier. I am going to look for a new job. Whatever it is, don't sit in it – use it to improve yourself.

Journal – Positive affirmations

Now it is your turn. Write down some positive affirmations that would mean something to you.

-
-
-
-
-

What am I going to say to myself to increase my self-belief, self-worth? What am I going to do to increase this?

Consider the 'I am' statement discussed earlier. Around the diagram below, make some statements which can positively reflect your character and create positive and uplifting thoughts.

I AM

Negative Ruminations

Whilst considering the above, it is also important that we continue to recognise those thoughts and feelings that are not serving us. Therefore, as another gentle reminder, consider the below:

What shit story/stories am I going to stop telling myself daily?

_____
_____
_____
_____
_____
_____

What am I going to do instead to make positive change?

_____
_____
_____
_____
_____
_____

If you are still struggling with this exercise, I still want you to use this lesson to positively serve you.

Perhaps try listening to some affirmations on YouTube and see how you find that as an exercise.

Sometimes, when I feel my thoughts falling down a

slippery path, I use positive affirmations, or 'self-talk', to steer them in a better direction.

"Come on, Joe, get your shit together, you got this, focus on how you want to feel."

Or if I find myself doubting myself or my abilities, I try use positive affirmations, or self-talk, to motivate myself. 'I can' do this.

It might sound crazy to a lot of people, but it positively serves me.

Use your journal to write some positive and uplifting stuff.

STOP YOUR SELF-LIMITING BELIEFS

> "The worst of all beliefs are self-limiting beliefs.
> If you believe yourself to be limited in some way, whether or not it's true, it becomes true for you. If you believe it, you will act as if you were deficient in that particular area of talent or skill. Overcoming self-limiting beliefs or self-imposed limitations is often the biggest obstacle standing between you and the realisation of your full potential."
>
> Unknown

Continuing from the above, I feel another negative concept that needs to be eliminated is that of 'self-limiting beliefs', which I feel unfortunately happens to most of us.

Consider me: as I considered my step into writing this, I was hit with a huge self-limiting belief – who the fucking hell am I to write a book? (So, I did a project instead, remember?)

However, in my own head, I already envisioned critics saying the same thing. "Who is this guy to give advice? He isn't a psychologist," or, "He doesn't run a multimillion-pound business," or, "He hasn't overcome certain types of life events that can truly define him as a person." "He isn't a SAS soldier or a major event survivor." "He isn't a former professional athlete or a movie superstar." I am pretty much an 'average Joe' to most, which is why I claimed the status of being 'Joe Bloggs' and why I wanted to make reference to it in the title. I am proud of writing it full stop, regardless of the outcome. It is also why I made reference to it in my business. I do see myself as an 'everyday' guy and that is OK; we can still want to better ourselves. I have big visions for my future. I allowed for 'self-belief' to prevail over 'self-limiting belief', and you must do the same.

As said previously, our minds will literally give us thousands of reasons why we can't do something – an inner critic who really wants to spoil the party. This clearly happened to me, as shown above, but it is about fighting to overcome this and, put simply, starting to believe in ourselves and not be beaten by our own self-defeating thoughts.

Therefore, I had to write this book. Even if it is viewed as utter garbage, I still did it. Even if it sells two copies, I still achieved it. Do not fear failure (another topic to come later).

You may be someone who suffers from your own self-limiting beliefs. You may be someone who does not. You may be someone who recognises their own self-limiting beliefs and tries to challenge them, or you could be someone who recognises them but lives in fear of challenging them. At the same time, some people do not even recognise their own self-limiting beliefs. I was unaware of what they were until I became involved in self-development.

I want this task to explore this concept and identify self-limiting beliefs to see how we can start to overcome them. The first step is to recognise them, and then you can create the principles to challenge them.

Becoming aware of your thoughts (and belief patterns in this case) is a massive breakthrough in personal development, as it allows you to analyse them with a level-headed approach. This is, again, why I believe in journaling so much, as it allows you to get everything out on a piece of paper in front of you. You are in a much better position to break down these thoughts constructively and start forming new belief patterns which will better serve you.

Journal — Challenging self-limiting beliefs

I want you to start by thinking of some current self-limiting beliefs you think are holding you back.

One exercise is to write down your limiting beliefs, cross them out and write the new belief you want to acquire.

This works similar to the 'switching gears' technique discussed earlier.

Taken from www.vetharmony.co.uk and adapted slightly.

It's about changing a 'limiting belief' to an 'empowering belief'

Limiting belief	Empowering belief
"I have never been good at…"	"I am capable of…"

_____

Cross the negative belief pattern out. Use this as a visual sign that you will no longer hold on to this belief pattern. The above is another simple but effective concept.

We can leave it here or we can go deeper in challenging our belief patterns if we so wish. This achieved through asking ourselves better questions and then journaling about our honest answers.

Look at one of your belief patterns and consider the following questions as you journal.

1. Why do you believe this? Where has this belief come from? Try to think back to one of the earliest experiences of this belief emerging. It could be from your upbringing, school or even later years. It could be something more recent.
2. What evidence is there to support this belief? (Use my beliefs surrounding publishing this book… they were all made up! My thoughts believed it! The truth is I could receive criticism, but at this stage there is no evidence to suggest it's true. Look into your own belief and assess it constructively.)
3. What has holding on to this limiting belief cost you? You may or may not be aware of this. However, confront it with honesty. Doing so helps motivate you to change. Answers could be: it's cost you money, health or self-respect, or relationships with people who matter to you. Perhaps it's stopping you being your best self. In my instance, listening to my limiting beliefs would have stopped me from ever publishing this book.
4. How has holding on to this limiting belief benefited you? (This may seem strange, but often we attach ourselves to the stories we tell as they provide comfort of some sort; it may give us an easier life – for example, in my case I wouldn't have to potentially face rejection or criticism and go on simply never knowing if the book would go on to do well.)
5. Am I willing to stop limiting myself? Yes or no. Think of

who you could be if you let go of these limiting thoughts. How you could develop personally and progress. Write down a new belief and start embracing this, start taking actions based on this.

Again, using my situation as an example, in my instance, I have now chosen yes. I am not going to let my limiting beliefs restrict me; I am going to keep pushing on with writing this book because it's something I want to do.

You can apply the above to any self-limiting beliefs and really help uncover them, which will hopefully lead to positive change.

Also use this area to add any extra notes you may have from the section above.

STOP WORRYING,
getting angry or upset about matters out of your control

> "Controlling life is like counting soap bubbles in the bath: it never ends and you end up wrinkly."
>
> Steve Errey

Another bit of guidance to live a better life is stop trying to control everything; sometimes we have to just let things be.

Is this easy? Do I get this perfect? Absolutely not. People still have to give me this advice sometimes, just less frequently now. Worrying about things out of our control can be seriously exhausting.

In the already highlighted book *Life's Amazing Secrets* by Gaur Gopal Das, the author states that we should complete a flowchart, which he claims eventually leads all arrows to 'why worry'.

Start with "Do I have a problem?" at the top. If the answer is no, then why worry? If the answer is yes, then there's another question: "Can I do something about it?" If the answer is yes, then why worry? If the answer is no, then why worry?

Perhaps this can be criticised as too simple a concept when we feel we have more sincere problems. What this concept is trying to emphasise is that if you can do something about your problem, then you don't really have a problem. If you can't, then you don't have one either, because the matter is out of your hands.

This isn't to say that you shouldn't attempt to solve the problems that you do have, but if there is truly nothing that can be done at that stage, then stop draining yourself.

Some things we worry about are completely out of our control. Yet, despite this, we chew ourselves up and hinder our times of enjoyment. We must try and learn to let such situations go, and as a result, we will feel less worried, less stressed and have more moments of joy.

In order to follow the 'why worry' ethos, also ask yourself a question concerning a situation you are in. "Is this within my control?" If it is not, then why waste your time dragging yourself down. I have been there! Stuck in traffic and sending myself into an angry rage. Being on holiday and having the unfortunate event of bad weather. There are thousands of examples. However, when we start recognising there are certain situations that we cannot control, it allows us to become less worried about them and to stop them from stealing our joy in those moments. It is another breakthrough in our personal development.

CHOOSE HOW YOU REACT TO A SITUATION

> "When you can't control what's happening, challenge yourself to control the way you respond to what's happening. That's where your power is."
>
> Unknown

This is a quote that also brings a lot of truth. The power is in how we choose to respond to a situation. I once heard this broken down in the following example. During a major traffic jam on a main motorway in the UK, two people's reactions were caught on live television. One gentleman was caught in a complete state of rage, anger and utter distress. Whilst on the opposite spectrum, a lady was seen to take her towel out of the car, lay it over her bonnet and begin sunbathing!

Now I'll grant that both could have been on the motorway for different reasons and had different levels of stress at the time; however, as a point, it holds a lot of truth.

I first saw this written by Jack Canfield, and it was referred to as 'Event + Response = Outcome'.

You can start to practise this in everyday life. Now when you know a moment happens to you that would perhaps cause a typical reaction, pause on it, think and then try to react differently.

To separate what you can control and what you cannot, the first thing you have to ask yourself is simply, "What can I control in this situation?" It allows you to understand the situation.

Without a doubt, though, you do have control over your mindset and your actions, and choosing to react more positively is going to have a better effect on your wellbeing.

Journal

As an exercise, I now want you to draft out this theory in practice. Think of a situation which has affected you previously, which was out of your control, which you did not deal with well. At the time you may not have even recognised this as out of your control. However, moving forward it will help you consider things from a different perspective.

This could be a situation at work, with a partner – there are so many situations it can happen in.

Make a list of these situations and make a commitment to yourself that you are going to let these go.

Think 'Event + Response = Outcome' and consider how you might react differently next time.

CHOOSE HOW YOU REACT TO A SITUATION

Event:

Previous Response	New Response

Previous Outcome	New Outcome

It may be that you cannot think of anything in this instance. That is OK. However, next time you find yourself wanting to react negatively to a situation, stop and consider what control you have over the situation; it could help how you react in the future.

Also use this area to add any extra notes you may have from the section above.

LEARN TO LIVE IN THE 'PRESENT MOMENT'
(The Power of Now by Eckhart Tolle)

"Realise deeply that the present moment is all you have.
Make this the primary focus of your life."
"Time isn't precious at all because it is an illusion."

Eckhart Tolle

This is a book I always have to go back to. I will not do this book justice in such a short space, but I would highly recommend it. I have been guilty of spending a lot of time, like a lot of people, worrying about the future and sitting on the past. I also have this weird struggle with the concept of time, whereby I hate 'wasting' it. This book goes into a spiritual level of appreciating the moment. Whenever I read it and go back to it and really try to focus on the present, I do feel my mood shifting from one of stress and worry to one of appreciation and gratitude.

The concept, in my understanding, is that we are often

entirely blind to small moments of goodness. When we are open to them, and we consciously start trying to recognise them, we can have more moments of joy. This could be something as simple as enjoying your favourite food or a cup of coffee, listening to your favourite song, enjoying a relaxing soak in the bath. It could be anything. Yet so many of us fail to take in such moments. Sometimes we are literally not even there; we could sit looking at a beautiful sunset whilst having our mind completely consumed by something else (again, I have done this countless times).

We tend to live in the past and the future. One moment we're reminiscing or regretting something, the next we're planning or worrying. If we can learn to be present more often, it is a great personal breakthrough. I personally do believe in good planning, and we will come to this later, but I also appreciate more moments of joy now.

In his book, Tolle states that there are no advantages to worrying about the future or dwelling in the past. Only the present is important because nothing ever occurs in the past or future; things happen only in a continuous stream of present moments. There are many positives to living 'in the now'; you will have more feelings of intense joy when carrying out activities you would perhaps dismiss or not truly recognise.

If you manage to achieve living in the now, you'll experience no major problems, just small ones that can be dealt with as they arise.

Give it a try, aim to live in the present more often. Stop clinging to the past and stop fearing the future; your life could improve dramatically and you can treasure those small moments of joy.

Journal – Mindfulness

I want you to practise being in the 'now'. Trust me, this process is hard at first, and I am not claiming to be someone who now walks round in a 'zen' state (as friends have jokingly stated about me). I do not preach this as if I have truly mastered this art. I have not 'mastered' anything; I just have more resources available to me now, for me to work with and practise.

But, becoming aware of being more present, and trying to apply it more often, certainly does lead you to enjoying moments more. Often moments you would overlook.

I want you to take in exactly what you are doing and appreciate this very moment. Perhaps you are sitting in your living room reading this with your family surrounding you. Perhaps you are commuting on the way to work and are surrounded by strangers. I don't know; the possibilities could be endless. However, wherever you are right now, I want you to stop for a moment and really take it in.

Yes, I know, again, you might feel fucking stupid if you have never done this before. However, it works.

- The colours, noises and surroundings. What can you see? What can you hear? What emotions are you feeling? What can you perhaps taste? I want you to jot it down. (Even if its on your phone).

LEARN TO LIVE IN THE 'PRESENT MOMENT'

If you are struggling with this exercise, try it elsewhere. Next time you are enjoying a coffee, eating your favourite food, exercising, taking a shower or engaging in an activity that you do not normally give much thought, try and really focus on it. It makes food taste better. It makes a shower even nicer. Stop and appreciate the moment.

If you get into the habit of this, you will start getting more moments of 'contentment' and little moments of joy.

GUIDANCE SURROUNDING LEARNING

Why learning is so vital to self-development and what you can do to improve yours.

Moving on to the next area in the book, I felt it was appropriate to highlight the importance of being an open learner in the process of self-development.

NEVER STOP LEARNING

> "Develop a passion for learning. If you do, you will never cease to grow."
>
> Anthony J D'Angelo

As human beings, we are gifted an opportunity to learn continuously. In addition to this, we are raised in a century where the opportunities to learn are endless so we must be sure to take full advantage.

We all learn in a variety of ways and I won't delve into this specifically; however, the fundamental is that we must always be open to learning new information.

I'm sure you have all heard the saying 'you learn something new every day'. While this may not be necessarily true for all, it certainly can be.

You could be a businessman at the top of your industry, but you should always be willing to listen to others to progress your skill level.

Or you could be simply trying to learn a new skill;

whatever it is, there are so many resources out there, and more often than not, they are free.

For me, this now applies to self-development and this is now a long-term life commitment. I will continuously seek to learn new skills that can benefit me. My whole life is now going to be a continuous study, and that excites me. I can view life as a continuous learning curve, which is much more appealing than seeing it as an almighty failure.

If you want to make positive changes and progress forward, you must be willing to learn.

> "If you wish to be successful, study success; if you wish to be happy, study happiness; if you wish to be wealthy, study wealth — don't leave it to chance, make it a study. You have to study the things that can change your economic, social, spiritual and personal life."
>
> Jim Rohn

Make it a daily habit. What am I going to learn today that I can use to develop my skills?

If you hear something great that really inspires you, or you read something great, highlight it, jot it down (in your journal) so you can go back to it. It may just inspire something great from you.

Like food can nourish our bodies, continued learning nourishes our minds. Learning new things can boost your profile at work; increase your confidence with skill; it can give you a sense of accomplishment. Learning is a core need for psychological wellbeing.

HAVE THE RIGHT ATTITUDE TO LEARNING
(growth vs fixed mindset)

> "The most important attitude that can be formed is that of desire to go on learning."
>
> John Dewey

I feel in order to develop personally, we must seize the opportunity to learn, and I believe that order to do this, we must focus on having the right mindset to learning.

Carol Dweck speaks of two mindsets. Those with a 'growth mindset' think of life as a learning process in which they can improve their capabilities and grow as individuals. "If at first you don't succeed, try then try again."

Those with a 'fixed mindset' believe they are stuck with whatever capabilities they have and no amount of practise can change this. It can be demonstrated well from the table below.

Fixed mindset	Growth mindset
Failure is the limit of my abilities	I learn from failure and it is an opportunity to grow
I am either good at it or I am not	I can learn anything I put my mind to
I don't like to be challenged	Challenges help me grow
When I am frustrated, I give up	My effort and attitude determine my abilities
I stick to what I know	I am open to new things
I cannot do it	I am willing to try

Have a completely open mindset to new things. See conversations as an opportunity to learn and not compete. Try to take a philosophical approach.

Thousands of years after his death, the ancient philosopher Socrates is still considered one of the wisest men who ever lived.

> "I am the wisest man alive, for I know one thing, and that is that I know nothing."
> Socrates

This was a driving force in his conversations and his openness to learning. Keep wanting to learn and better yourself.

So, don't be a know it all, be open and you could just learn something great.

TOOLS TO LEARN
positive audiobooks/YouTube videos/podcasts and books – more importantly, make notes!

So the last tip I discussed was to never stop learning; this next section focuses on immersing ourselves in this.

We live in a world where we have so many options available to us. It is fantastic.

YouTube videos, podcasts and audiobooks are an easy start. When you go to scream, "Fuck you!" and shout at the car that just cut you up, but you suddenly hear the line, "Today, I will be **positive**," blaring from your car speakers, it makes it a little bit harder. Which again highlights the point that positive thinking will serve us more than negative thinking will.

It didn't seem too difficult to ease into this. I didn't even know what 'positive psychology' was at the time I began this journey. I think I searched for things such as 'How to stop feeling like shit' on YouTube in my desperate plea for help.

For anyone new to this: search for the buzzwords discussed

throughout and watch your world open to something you never knew existed. There is just so much material out there; I am only scratching the surface.

There are so many podcasts available and audiotapes about whatever topic you wish to listen to.

Search for specific motivational speakers. Some of my favourites have included: Tony Robbins/Les Brown/Mel Robbins/Jim Rohn/Jordan Peterson – but there are so many!

Your morning commute can go from being one of complete stress and negative emotions to being a mobile university. It can make commuting enjoyable.

Make sure you make regular learning a habit.

> "Reading is to the mind what exercise is to the body."
> Joseph Addison

I can't stress enough the importance of reading. I found online after a pretty basic Google search that a recent survey by Fast Company suggests the average number of books read by a CEO is sixty books per year or five books each month. I don't know how precisely accurate this is (it's not my job to go into full depth here), but the point is that I can guarantee you must read a lot. It allows you to stay ahead of the game and move forwards. So if you're in business, then get reading. If you want to stay positive, get reading.

For me, reading positive books fills my mind with positive material. There are so many fantastic books out there. There are now apps which digest books into smaller reads summarising their main content. Utilise these. Now, if I am waiting to get my haircut, instead of spending all my time on social media, I will read a book!

If you don't currently read, start small! Make a commitment to read a chapter of a self-development book daily. Try it and see if it helps you feel better as you start to learn new and exciting information.

Journal

As well as having a good desire to learn, I think planning your learning can be a good way to ensure you set yourself up correctly. There is so much information out there; it can sometimes feel like you are swamped. Planning your learning can be a good tool to avoid this. In addition to this, we want to retain the information and put it to good use, which is why journaling can be a vital skill for ensuring you have something to refer back to.

Don't let all your hard work become 'shelf help', whereby you read it, put the book down and never revisit it. Digest the work into small note form that you can always reflect on. This is what I did.

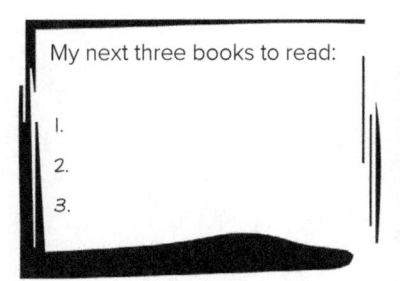

My next three books to read:

1.
2.
3.

My next three key speakers to listen to:

1.
2.
3.

My next three audiobooks will be:	My next three podcasts will be:
1.	1.
2.	2.
3.	3.

Once you have started reading more books, make a note of the key points. Journal about them. Ask yourself some questions around what you have read – it could be something as basic as:
- What are the key points I took from this week's learning?
- What information can I start applying today?

This is another reason why your notebook/journal is your best asset. This information is always there for you to reflect back on!

START JOURNALING

> "A personal journal is an ideal environment in which to 'become', it is a perfect place for you to think, feel, discover, expand, remember and dream."
>
> Brad Wilcox

So throughout this whole book there have been areas for you to journal and make notes, and I have kept referring to it throughout. It is important to explain a little bit more.

When I was first introduced to the concept of journaling, my immediate reaction was to put on macho bravado and laugh it off. "There is no chance I am writing a 'diary'… I am not a five-year-old girl," was something close to my response.

However, now I would encourage everybody to do it.

The concept of journaling can be done in many ways, but it is an essential component of learning and self-development.

It can be done to practise gratitude, to note down your accomplishments for that day, to make a note of what you wish to achieve tomorrow. It can be completely unique to you.

I also soon came to realise that a journal, for me, became my creative platform and my motivational diary. If I was having moments of stress, challenging situations or even feeling low, I could open my journal and read some of the positive content in there that I had read. Not only that, but the material I was writing also became my source writing this book. I was reading so much and taking in so much content as it was growing, I had to find another place for it all to fit, so I put it into this. As I have said, my journal was essentially becoming my counsellor.

Use it for inspiration. Your next business idea might come from it.

It doesn't always have to be a 'journal'; make it a 'business brainstorm book', and your next amazing idea might come there. How many thoughts and ideas do we let go a day and then forget about? You may just have your next big idea which you can jot down.

I have also used a journal like a 'training diary', used for my Thai boxing and in the gym. I can note down certain drills or exercises. It has so many applications to it. I truly believe in having a small notebook that you carry with you daily. You can even incorporate everything if you wish.

I know most people would say it is 2021 and we can do it all on our phone or on an app, etc., but the power of a journal should not be underestimated.

BE YOUR OWN COUNSELLOR
and rid yourself of negativity

– 'kvetching and rapid writing' (Write It Down Make It Happen by Henriette Anne Klauser)

Following on from above, I keep saying this book has essentially become my own counsellor. I would write about my feelings whilst searching for answers through various platforms. This became my little book of guidance. It was my way of desperately trying to find myself and fulfilment on the way. In the above book, the author talks of a Jewish tradition known as 'kvetching', which is a way of talking through your feelings and getting rid of anger and resentment, which is said to help get rid of negativity. It is expected that it would start as a horrible tirade, but afterwards, you will feel much better and hopefully have some answers to your problems.

She speaks of a similar concept of 'rapid writing' to help power through mental blocks. As suggested, this involves quick non-stop writing; in such a technique, you never look back at what you have written and you just keep going. Like kvetching, after a few pages and the bottled-up negativity being released, it is hoped that the solution starts to present itself clearly. It is said to be a method to access the deep recesses of your mind. By applying such a technique, it can help you identify fears and worries and make realistic strategic plans to remove them.

'Rapid writing' can also become a source of creativity – again, like journaling, doing such a thing allows you to turn ideas into reality.

I think of writing as taking my brain to the 'tip yard' – I know this sounds a bit strange, but it's a place for me to completely unload. I can get my feelings and thoughts out, but it helps me learn further by documenting what I have already taken in.

I believe that by getting everything down on paper, you almost see things like you are an outsider looking in. I would often describe my head as 'fuzzy' when I had too much going on. Sometimes I could not process everything as it felt overwhelming. However, as soon as this was out on paper for me to see visually, I was able to process them much more constructively.

There are so many benefits to 'journaling' in whatever way you choose to use it, which is why I keep encouraging you to carry a small notebook with you, as it will serve you so well.

GUIDANCE TO BE MORE POSITIVE

Simple, really — a number of ways in which you can boost positivity. My favourite advice on helping you to achieve this.

Moving on, we now understand why we need more positive thoughts and words and less negative ones. I now want to talk about some concepts which are going to hopefully help get you being the best version of you and ways to get into a healthier state of mind.

BE THE BEST VERSION OF YOURSELF
(Best Self by Mike Bayer)

In trying to ensure you are always your best, most positive self, I wanted to start by giving some guidance read from the author stated here. This is something I have adapted now myself to suit my own version.

He explains we all have two types of self: a positive best self (this is the person you'd like to be more often, the person who makes you feel good about being you) and a negative anti-self which stops you from being that person.

Perhaps you dislike the version that loses their temper or overindulges in alcohol or eats too much bad food. This will happen from time to time, but Bayer states that the key is to learn to tell which self is in control. He says the best way to do that is to flesh out these characters and give them recognisable attributes (by drawing them on a piece of paper). I will be honest, I don't do the drawing part; I don't have to, as the textual stuff works for me, but I love the concept.

Method

- Positive self:
  On a piece of paper, you write down all of your positive traits: the things you admire most about yourself, but you don't always act upon.

- Negative self:
  Repeat what you did with your best self, but instead, write down everything you dislike about your behaviour when your anti-self is in charge.

Now think of five recent situations when your anti-self was in control. Write down how it behaved and then compare it to what your best self would've done.

As stated, the author above has a version whereby he draws the characters (feel free to apply this method). I don't do this. However, I do pin this best-self textual version on my self-development board (or pop it in my journal), so that I can see the version I would prefer to be.

It might seem strange at first, but reminding yourself of your 'better version' self is going to increase your chances of being that person.

It may make you feel uncomfortable at first. However, getting out of your comfort zone is an essential element to personal growth (more to come later).

You might try it and think, Yeah, this absolutely does not work for me, but give it a go at least.

Even if you only pin up your 'best self' version of yourself or you write the characteristics of your best self in your journal, this is something to aim for.

This 'best self' can be related to any area of your life. I previously used it to look at my previous regular activity of excessive binge drinking. I wrote 'in control' and 'blind drunk', and surrounded the topic with insightful words. My drinking habits have improved as a result of this.

I can now use this method in other areas of my life, such as business, relationships and day-to-day life.

Important point: You may fuck up again on occasions as you try to improve yourself... This is OK, and you should not punish yourself too much as a result of it. Be motivated that you are trying to make positive changes.

Journal – Attribute of yourself:

Worst self key qualities:	Best self key qualities:
•	•
•	•
•	•
•	•
•	•
•	•
•	•
•	•
•	•
•	•
•	•
•	•

The key areas in which you would like to apply your best self:

QUOTES/PERSONAL MANTRAS
– 'quote of the day'

When it comes to seeing influential quotes, I used to be that person judging others for writing them and I would roll my eyes. What a dickhead! was my typical first thought (sad but true).

I now know though that they can have a positive influence. I post them almost daily across social media. For some people, they often have a quote or a mantra that has stuck with them over time, and a lot of individuals use these quotes to help guide them in life, or they serve as being a huge influence on how they act. We often see them on business walls or in gyms as motivation.

In terms of lifting my mood, I have found it very useful is to write a 'quote of the day', and this is something I applied at home. I would write something on the chalkboard downstairs, which I would read before leaving the house; did I change the world as a result of this? No, not quite. However, it could help me leave home feeling upbeat or grateful. This solely depends on what the quote represented.

This has also been taken further and is something I transferred to the workplace, and although it's not for everybody, it can have a positive impact on some.

I also have quotes as my phone background, which can often reflect a way I am feeling or something I wish to remind myself of.

I have quotes on my vision board. I have quotes in my journal. I have quotes everywhere. Quotes will not do the work for us, but they can serve us positively and give us a little boost. I now really like inspiring quotes.

Mantra

As for mantras, I have seen people have complete focus and direction because of a mantra they follow.

What is a mantra? A personal mantra is an affirmation to motivate and inspire you to be your best self. The purpose is to provide motivation and encouragement to you when you need to focus your mind on achieving a goal.

Again, businesses may use this as motivation to embed their values with their products.

Other people use it as a complete guide for their motivation in life. I once heard that Will Smith used the words 'improve lives' to motivate himself in a lot of his work. This is powerful. If you have a burning desire to push something or have an idea, find your mantra. It allows you to ask yourself daily, is this striving towards my mantra? Is the work I am doing reflecting the message I am trying to spread? If it is not, then you know you need to change something; if it is, then you know you're on the right path.

A guy called Davie McConnachie (DMC Fitness), whom I watched on a two-day mindset course, had a mantra of 'Strength for Life', and he used this within his business for his gym and he also used it to spread positive and motivating content online and through seminars. To him, this guides him and gives his work a purpose and a meaning. It was extremely powerful and the whole concept of it is inspiring. He is an extremely motivating character.

I personally always tell myself to 'keep g(r)o(w)ing'. Now I don't mean in height. No matter what obstacles life throws at us, we can always keep going forward and we can always keep growing on a personal level. Because I suffered so much with my own thoughts previously, I can use this as a guide to keep me on track and remind me of the importance of engaging in my self-development and mindset work. Even if something feels tough now and it doesn't feel like we will see the finish line, keep working on you (keep growing), keep moving forward, filling your mind with healthy, positive material. This will serve you so much more than negativity will.

In my business, I use the mantra of 'inspire, motivate, change', and these three powerful words serve as a positive reminder to make sure that each day I am pushing these principles to help serve others.

Journal — Quotes and mantras

I now want you to write some quotes that inspire you. If you don't yet have them, I want you to seek them out. Aim for seven so you have one for each day of the week.

Find quotes related to different areas of your life, health and wellness, business or career, relationships etc. or simply anything that motivates you to push forwards.

Your quotes:

1.
2.
3.
4.
5.
6.
7.

Mantra

I also want you to think of something you would use as a daily mantra, something to live your life by, that is going to inspire you to be the best version of yourself each day.

BE NICE TO ONE ANOTHER AND GIVE TO OTHERS

> *"When we help ourselves, we find moments of happiness; when we help others, we find lasting fulfilment."*
>
> Simon Sinek

I once heard the saying 'We are all crewmates on the same ship'.

And this resonated with me a lot. In relation to wellbeing, we often don't know what someone else is going through, so just try your best to be nice to one another.

In doing so, you will find more happiness for yourself as well. It also doesn't have to be a great huge gesture; it can be something small.

Tony Robbins describes two things that will make us feel alive, and that is 'growing' and 'giving'. This is what is truly required to be happy. Therefore, in terms of altruism (how giving is described), it could be argued that this is one of the most important take-home messages from this book.

I have done several things over the years, which have included donating to food banks, donating Christmas gifts to underprivileged children, buying the homeless a coffee, to name a few. These are hardly bank-breakers, but each time I did them, I felt good.

It's also not something I do all the time (these acts are quite sparse). I am not portraying myself as some of saint here in any way shape or form. However, put simply, it is a nice feeling to help someone out occasionally. Also don't be that person who needs to plaster it on social media; such nice gestures can be done quietly.

You may not be in the position to give things away, but try your best to do something nice for someone. Altruism doesn't need to be a huge gesture. Stop and hold the door for someone next time you are out shopping. Help a friend out with something they need a hand with. Give a friend your time to listen to their worries and offer support. If anything, just be more patient with people. This is something we can do more often and I try to do more frequent acts of small gestures.

We often see bitterness in life from people who have felt hard done by. They make a pact to never be there for anyone else ever again. I have said myself, sometimes we must be selfish in the pursuit of our dreams, and I do genuinely believe that. However, it can always feel good to help someone else. The truth is, you might not get the favour returned, but try not to look at it with such bitterness, as you have still done something great and it says a lot about your character.

There is something that is known as the 'helper's high';

this is another name for the uplifting feeling that people experience after doing a good deed or act of kindness. This high is rooted in natural instincts to help our fellow humans. It could be argued that altruism is slightly 'selfish' because there is no denying that it makes us feel good, but the other person benefits too, meaning there are two winners.

Also, remember that people can be unkind and ungrateful; it is just part of being human. Instead, take joy from knowing you have done the kind act yourself.

The reason altruism can be so beneficial is that it gives meaning to our lives and connects us with other people. It is a huge part of personal development in my eyes. Like I said, it doesn't need to be something material; it can be something as simple as lending a hand to a friend.

In the *Happiness Hypothesis* book by Jonathan Haidt, the author pays tribute to a study which found that old people who offered their help to others lived a longer and happier life than old people who merely received such support. So, it seems to be pretty good for our health as well.

Journal

Note some ideas of acts of altruism that you can do, which will help others:

Record what you do:

Keep a kindness record. There are a million nice things you can do to help someone out. It doesn't have to cost a great deal of money, but it can still make you feel great.

If you're having a shit day, remind yourself of some of the good things you have done for others (keep it in your journal). As well as this, by engaging in an act of kindness it will no doubt lift your mood to.

CHANGE YOUR STATE

I also wanted to discuss the concept of 'changing our state'. This is a theory that I learned from the master Tony Robbins and it has been re-edited time and time again by many others.

As I am not a psychologist, I don't want to delve too deep with this one. However, too often, we feel we are powerless to our emotions when this is simply untrue. We can change our moods. We can change our state.

State of mind refers to 'your mood or mental state at a particular time' (Collins Dictionary).

Synonyms include: attitude, perspective, outlook, approach.

One way to change our mental state is to move our body. Our physiology can change our biology. Our body language sends signals to our brains; therefore, something as simple as adjusting our posture can produce a more positive state. Exercise is another fantastic way to change our state.

Breathing. This is a way to calm your emotions and see things from a different perspective.

There are many other ways to change our state. Feeling stressed or upset? Go for a walk through nature. Play some upbeat music... have a dance if you so wish (again, movement).

What we chose to focus on also affects our state of mind. As Tony says, "Where focus goes energy flows," so if we notice something that is not serving us, we can take our attention away from it and focus it on something new.

If we are always picking out flaws or paying attention to our negative aspects, this will influence how we feel. This is where demonstrating gratitude and appreciation is going to serve us more.

There will be occasions where you are choosing to hold on to things. You had a fight with your partner, and you choose to focus on that and remain angry for the remainder of the day. This is going to affect your day and how you feel.

Am I saying I never do this now? Absolutely not. I am not perfect. However, I am fully aware that I can choose to change the way I feel. I also know that if I found a way to change my state, it would leave me feeling different about the situation.

START SMILING MORE
...say hello to strangers

"Life is short, smile while you still have teeth."

Unknown

This might appear a bit cheesy, I know… I was even going to leave this out of the book, as I thought I was going down the 'soppy' route slightly with it. However, I love this advice and yet it is so simple. Now I am not expecting everyone to go around with big fake smiles on their faces or grinning at any opportunity, but in moments you see fit, have a little smile.

At one of my previous places of work, my boss used to walk in every morning and say, "Good morning, campers," with a big smile on her face and it really can make such a difference. Think about a moment a stranger has smiled at you; it can leave a pretty good impact. If a stranger looks at you and smiles, say hello. The final touches were put on this book during the COVID-19 pandemic (2020), when the rules started easing and we were able to go out for exercise. I was running past people in the street saying hello to every stranger I saw; I loved it. Yes, it was in a time of crisis, but it certainly made me feel better and I imagine it didn't have a negative impact on them either.

Smiling can trick your brain into happiness and actually boost your health; it is said to spur a chemical reaction in your brain that can make you feel happier, and science has shown that it can lift your mood, lower stress, boost your immune system and possibly even prolong your life. It relates to changing your body language and state.

Try going around and smiling at people more. Say hello to strangers – you might just get a smile or a hello back. As my mam used to say as a kid, "It's nice to be nice."

GET RID OF TOXIC PEOPLE

This point is so important, and I cannot stress this enough.

Jim Rohn, in relation to his 'mental factory', talks about 'standing guard at your mental factory door with who you let in'. If you have people around you who are constantly negative or trying to bring you down, either decide to remove these people from your life or minimise the time spent with them. You should be surrounding yourself with people who uplift you or motivate you or encourage you to do things.

The easiest way to catch a cold is to hang around with somebody with a cold. The easiest way to catch a negative mindset is to hang about someone with a negative mindset.

Now let's be honest… we can try and be as positive as we want, but there will always be someone out there who wants to bring us down.

Unfortunately for a lot of people, they get a sense of pleasure in bringing others down and these people are everywhere. There is the infamous 'keyboard warrior', and we all know that one person at the social gathering who just cannot be happy for anybody. These people exist everywhere, and the harsh reality is that unfortunately, at some point in our lives, we have probably all met this person; we have likely been that person. I am also not going to sit here and say it is easy to often forget about some of the harsh things said by others, but we have to really try to.

My advice is to try not to waste your time and energy criticising other people or to dwell on being affected by other people.

The world needs more people who will build each other up or lift people's mood. You want to spend more of your time with these types of people.

Also, try to look at such people with a light-hearted perspective. I once heard on a Jim Rohn audiotape that there are only ten real nasty, miserable people in the world (it is just that they tend to move around a lot), so while this is obviously untrue, it is worth trying to have such a perspective. Every once in a while, you will bump into one of these people; however, when you do, you only have another nine to bump into. Whilst it is easier said than done, if we can teach ourselves not to rise to such people and become personally affected, then we will find ourselves more content.

I feel we sometimes live in a society where some people take pleasure in seeing other people fail or not being happy. It is very sad, but I believe it to be true. Always remember this: not everybody is like this, and for everyone who gives you this impression, there is someone out there who believes you are capable of great things. The best part about it all is that you can choose whether you become affected by such negative people. As Ghandi once said:

> *"I will not let anyone walk through my mind with their dirty feet."*

Which is quite a majestic quote from a world idol, and it holds so much truth.

Granted, I am not Ghandi, but simply remember that we can be selective of what information we choose to take on board. So, while it may hurt at the time or you may want to react in a certain way, try not to dwell on the situation. Choose how you wish to react. I am talking from experience; I have explained in this book how it used to affect me a hell of a lot and I struggled with it. However, it's really time to teach yourself to stop giving a fuck about other people's opinions when they're not served in a helpful way.

I once heard the saying that 'one negative fish can drain the oxygen of the whole fish tank', and while it can be true, we must choose to be better than that. If you consistently feel like someone is trying to drag you down, or saying consistently negative things, choose the time you wish to spend with them wisely, as it is only going to bring you negative energy. Yes, you can choose how you respond, but why the fuck would you choose to keep spending time with them? It's like pouring fuel on a fire. Surround yourself with people who can lift you up.

In addition to this, don't let negative people dictate your life or destroy your dreams.

Be aware of 'crab mentality'. It is a popular phrase used amongst Filipinos. This is a metaphor that is used to describe some very typical human behaviour. It is used to describe a way of thinking best described by the phrase, "If I can't have it, neither can you."

The metaphor refers to a pot of crabs. Individually, the crabs could easily escape from the pot, but instead, they grab at each other in a useless 'king of the hill' competition which prevents any of them from escaping and ensures their collective demise.

As an example, the bucket is your job, and you want to leave to try something new. Do your friends and co-workers encourage you to go for it or do they try and pull you back down to reality?

If you want to climb out of your 'bucket', whatever it may be, don't let the other crabs pull you down. If you're happy in your bucket but see someone else making a break for it, give them a helping hand; they might help you too.

DO NOT BE THAT NEGATIVE PERSON!
Stop being a dick

Excuse the language. I will keep this short and sweet. In the same context as all the above, it is also essential that we ourselves try not to be the constant negative person that is constantly draining the fucking life out of people. Try and be happy for people. Make sure you celebrate when the people you love do well for themselves.

As stated, I am not Ghandi or a great philosopher. So, in 'Joe Bloggs' terms, stop being a dickhead to other people or talking so much shit (gossiping)! I am not saying do not have an opinion on things as we all have values and beliefs and I believe in being able to express them. I am happy for a debate. What I mean here, though, is that it astonishes me at times how people can just blurt something out to someone so unnecessarily. They will try belittling them or embarrassing them (in front of others) for some reason, for example with what they are choosing to do in their life (remember the former schoolteacher... now he was a dickhead). Thankfully I have educated myself on how to react much better now.

I am not saying I have never had a moan about someone. I have put the world to rights in my eyes on many occasions (and I would be lying if I said this won't ever happen again), but the point I am trying to make is along the lines of:

> "Blowing someone else's candle out won't make yours shine any brighter."
> Unknown

In summary, it's often somebody's own shortcomings that makes them resort to this.

If you are consciously aware that this is something you do, consider trying to break this habit. Calling someone stupid won't make you any smarter. Ruining someone else's day won't make yours better. If you want to offer someone some guidance, offer them something constructively that they can work with. Point made on this one.

LIMIT YOUR INTAKE OF THE NEWS AND MEDIA

Have you ever considered just how many negative things come up on the news? It was only when I started to become conscious of this that I realised how negative the news and media could actually be. When you are constantly feeding your mind with negative messages, it becomes much more difficult to remain positive. Remember, it is our mental toolbox. Do we want our morning commute to be filled with all that is wrong with the world? Instead, substitute this with some positivity. An audiobook or even some uplifting music can help get your day off to a more positive start.

I am not saying you should cut the news out altogether; it may be that you want to know what is going on in the world. There are some really uplifting and positive news stories as well, which can be inspirational – focus on these. I do believe we should certainly look to limit our intake. For me, the media created fear and filled my mind with looking at the bad in the world; I had to consciously shift to start avoiding this. I choose which news articles I now read and as a result it affects me less.

SURROUND YOURSELF WITH POSITIVE PEOPLE
/assess your environment

"Be picky about who you keep around you, Personalities, words and traits do rub off naturally."

Sonya Teclair

In the opposite of surrounding yourself with negative people, start surrounding yourself with positive people. Again, if there is someone who is constantly dragging you down, are they worthy of your time?

Start spending time with people who lift you up, who offer you guidance and support, people who bring out the best in you and energise you. People who can be critical, but in a way that serves you.

Being with people who have your best interests at heart and want you to accomplish things in life is going to be much more beneficial than those who are not.

It can be motivating for you and influential, as well as ensuring you have a good support system. This skill comes down to assessing your environment. Find an environment in which you prosper. For a business, this could be networking events or seminars; for life, this could be with those special people who fill you with encouragement. Look around and really assess your environment… are you putting yourself in a place where you can best develop and grow as a person? Or are you around people continually bringing you down?

> "A shark in a fish tank will grow to be eight inches, but in the ocean, it will grow to eight feet or more. A shark will never outgrow its environment and the same is true about you. Change your environment and watch your growth accelerate."
>
> Unknown

Jim Rohn suggests that, "You are the average of the five people you spend most of your time with." Therefore, we should be choosing carefully where and with whom you are spending your time. Make sure your friends and family are encouraging you (as you should be encouraging them). You should only be creating room for those people who want the best for you. People who show genuine love and support for you.

If you want to make positive changes in your life, in whatever area that is, you need a supportive network.

LEARN TO BE GRATEFUL

> "If you look at what you have in life, you'll always have more. If you look at what you don't have in life, you'll never have enough."
>
> Oprah Winfrey

We always long for more. Again, I am not stating this as a negative trait. I salute the 'go-getters' who wake up motivated, positive to make a change and chase their goals and dreams. I take my hats off to them; such people inspire me. I use this to help boost my motivations; I use this to inspire me to finish this book! To push me on in my personal pursuits.

However, at the same time as this, it is so important that we also reflect on and value the things we do have in life.

Showing gratitude is one of the best things to do to start seeing positive change. It does not matter where you are in life; there will always be something that you can be grateful for.

Here is part of an inspiring Carl Burns quote to reflect that:

> *"Sometimes you are unsatisfied with your life, whilst many people in this world are dreaming of living your life…*
>
> *A child on a farm sees a plane fly overhead and dreams of flying. But, a pilot on the plane sees the farmhouse and dreams of returning home.*
>
> *That's life! Enjoy yours… If wealth is the secret to happiness, then the rich should be dancing on the streets. But only poor kids do that.*
>
> *If beauty and fame bring ideal relationships, then celebrities should have the best marriages."*

Gratitude has so many health benefits. It removes a multitude of negative emotions. By learning to stop and have moments of appreciation for what we do have in life, it can help to foster more positive wellbeing.

Journal – A gratitude task

One of the most common practices you will hear when it comes to gratitude is to write down three things every day that you are grateful for. This has been shown to have many health benefits.

Try to make it habitual, perhaps as part of a morning routine (details to follow) when you first wake up or just before you go to bed. Write it in your journal!

At this stage of this book, I want to take a moment to reflect on three things you are grateful for:

- _____
- _____
- _____

Do not just make it generic either. If you say family, why exactly are you grateful for your family. Uncover a little bit more meaning behind it. Try and make this habitual and it will help boost your wellbeing.

Idea – A gratitude message

Another task which can be of benefit is to send a gratitude message to someone who means a lot to you.

Let them know what they did, why you are grateful, how they affected your life. It could be a loved one or a friend. It will make their day.

Use this area to make any further notes or to draft a gratitude message.

GUIDANCE ON HELPING TO HEAL ANY MENTAL 'SCARS'
and to Move Forward in Life

This is for anyone who might be carrying some pain or struggling to let go of things. It gets a little bit 'deeper' in this section.

Introducing this section, I feel it is important to note that during life, as human beings, we will make mistakes and encounter situations where we will be hurt. I feel like a large part of self-development is learning to deal with such events to move forward. The following tips will hopefully shed some light on this.

LET GO OF PAST MISTAKES

> "There is no sense in punishing your future for the mistakes of your past, forgive yourself, grow from it and then let it go."
>
> Melanie Koulouris

I have made many mistakes in my past. I have had to learn to use these as a learning curve, all as part of my journey and personal growth.

The point is, a lot of us carry too much baggage with us each day, which can seriously weigh us down and stop us from moving forward.

However, as has been highlighted, the only real thing we can affect is what we are doing right now.

I have done a lot of things which, on reflection, were not good choices. I often upset family members with past behaviours and had numerous fallings-out over things. I have seriously let down friends as well as partners. I have been arrested on occasions and subsequently ended up with a four-page criminal record. I have reacted to situations in ways I wish I had not; I have made decisions I wish I had not. I will make mistakes in the future. (I am human.)

I still do not live a 'perfect life'; however, each day, I am always trying to make sure I am working on myself. As I have said, find me anyone who has the 'perfect' life – it is just not true.

In my eyes it is less about being the perfect you and more about being the best form of yourself. You must try not to keep hold of these past mistakes as they will leave you stewing over and over and can lead to negative traits of emotion.

In Japan, there is an art known as 'kintsugi', which involves using a precious metal such as liquid gold or silver to bring back together pieces of broken pottery while at the same time enhancing the breaks.

By repairing the broken ceramics, it's possible to give a new lease of life to the pottery, which now becomes even more refined thanks to its 'scars'. The idea is that broken objects are not something to hide but to display with pride. We shouldn't just throw away objects because they are broken; it doesn't mean that it is not useful anymore. We should try to repair things because sometimes in doing so we obtain more valuable objects than what we started with.

We need to apply this to our everyday lives; we can learn as individuals from negative experiences, and our 'scars' can make us a more desirable person in the long run.

We see this happening day to day in life…

Former drug addicts who now help others become drug-free…

Former gangsters who help keep young people out of trouble…

People who have carried so much pain and hurt to go on and live happily, content, successful lives…

It is similar to the post-traumatic growth discussed earlier.

I like to think of what I am doing as something similar. I want to use my experiences to help others.

This leads me to my next Jim Rohn point:

> *"It's not what happens that determines our future, it's what you do about what happens."*

He used the metaphor of the wind and a ship sail. He suggested that the same wind blows on us all. The wind of disaster, pain, hurt, opportunity.

It is not the blowing of the wind that determines our future but the set of the sail that determines our arrival.

Learning is all about setting the sail. The sail that you set today will determine your destination tomorrow. The choices you make from today can determine your future.

Remember, you cannot grow without a challenge! And your past is all part of the journey.

LET GO OF RESENTMENT

"Anger, resentment and jealousy doesn't change the heart of others – it only changes yours."

Shannon Alder

Let go of resentment – a wise piece of advice. How easy is this for me to say... Who the fuck am I to say this? I am not a psychologist. I don't know what's going on in your life or has happened in the past, and you are totally right.

Dr Wayne Dyer claims that, "There are no justified resentments." ...this is a very bold statement. At first glance, most will likely get defensive and disagree, and being truthful to myself, I have been the same. It is hard – I get it.

He goes on to say, no matter what anyone says to you, or what anger comes directed towards you, no matter how much hate you may encounter, there are no justified resentments. If you carry resentments about anything or anyone – the person you lent money to and didn't pay you back, the person who walked out on you and left you for someone else, and all the things you have justified that you have the right to be resentful about – then those resentments will only end up harming you and creating in you a sense of despair.

When it is put like this, it makes more sense. This is a big part of my personal development. There are things I have held on to much longer than I should (many, many times). I spent a lot of time hurting over what people had said to me. I spoke about this at the start; I struggled with it.

However, the truth is, why do we hold on to it? It is only causing us pain.

Dyer extends his argument with the following concept: nobody ever dies from a snake bite; a snake bite cannot kill you. You cannot be unbitten; once you are bitten, you are bitten, but it's the venom that continues to pour through your system after the bite that will end up destroying you. Linking this back to his statement about resentment, the fundamental truth is that you cannot move forward in life if you are feeling resentment against someone or something. If you let the venom continue to flow through your body and don't put a stop to it, you will not end up in a good place. The only one who fucking suffers is you. Definitely food for thought.

LEARN TO FORGIVE YOURSELF

> "Forgive yourself. The supreme act of forgiveness is when you can forgive yourself for all the wounds you've created in your own life. Forgiveness is an act of self-love. When you forgive yourself, self-acceptance begins and self-love grows."
>
> Miguel Angel Ruiz

Self-forgiveness is essential to self-healing. I have fucked up on many occasions, as we all have. I do not feel I have overcome any great adversity and I stated this at the beginning, but I have done things which have left me feeling nothing but pure hatred for myself. I have also done things that have seriously upset others.

Forgiveness can be one of the hardest things you have to do, and forgiving yourself is the hardest of all. It is more challenging than forgiving someone else because you live with yourself and your thoughts twenty-four seven. This can be a dangerous territory.

However, like resentment, not forgiving yourself is like picking at an open wound; the wound is there and this can't be changed, but how you react to it can be controlled. It is so much easier said than done, but emotionally healthy people must have the capacity to forgive themselves when they have made a mistake; otherwise, you cannot move forward.

This is not to say that if you have made a mistake, you should not reflect on your actions. We must use it as a learning curve. However, it is only when you forgive yourself when you make a mistake that it becomes easier to address the consequences of your actions productively.

SHOW YOURSELF SOME LOVE

"You're always with yourself, so you might as well enjoy the company."
Diane Von Furstenberg

Following on nicely from the previous advice, I must talk about self-love. When put in this context, it can seem like a bit of a 'wishy-washy' thing to talk about for a lot of people (especially men – including me), but it is essential.

In a YouTube video titled 'Oprah gifting WISDOM that she learned from a Life Coach', Oprah Winfrey says keeping your own self full is your job. Yet some people are afraid of 'being full of yourself'. However, it is only when you are like this that you can offer your full self to the rest of the world.

Life coach and speaker Christine Hasler says the relationship that you have with yourself is the most important relationship you can have. If it is unhealthy, it will impact everything in your life, and looking back, I had a toxic relationship with myself.

As humans, we all have these stories that we carry around like a heavy bag. As much as we want to change them, we can become attached to them. I am unlovable, I am not good enough and I'm broken. Life tends to reaffirm it. We believe it and life shows us everything to believe it.

Hasler says that if she spoke to her friends as she spoke to herself, she wouldn't have any. (Seriously, imagine it if you went up to your best friend and called them fucking useless or a failure – I don't imagine you would get a pleasant response... yet I was telling myself this stuff daily.)

So you have to stop the crazy mind chatter that tells you you're not good enough. This is a serious form of personal mental abuse and it's not going to have a healthy outcome. Go back to the positive affirmations section if required.

DO NOT BE AFRAID TO ASK FOR HELP

Taken from the book *Brave* by Margie Warrell, she highlights that if you require support, it is critical that you ask for help. Too many of us have been conditioned to believe that asking for help is a sign of weakness, but it should be recognised as a sign of strength. It is brave to display your vulnerability to others and should be seen as an act of courage.

Asking others for help will introduce you to the power of community. Most people (not all) are likely to help somebody else in a time of need. So don't be afraid to ask for help; it certainly is not a weakness. This could be something as simple as asking for some assistance with a project at work you're struggling with, to more serious concerns such as your mental health. For me, my first counsellor visit (my 'real life' counsellor, and not my journal) was one of the most important steps in my own life. I asked for help and I am a better person as a result of it. I was tremendously nervous at first (I felt it challenged my masculinity and I was uncomfortable), but now I speak about it with pride in the hope it might help others. Also remember support can be in many forms (friends, family, support groups) and it doesn't always have to be related to mental health. I just wish that more people could understand that it's ok to ask for help or support.

GUIDANCE TO IMPROVE PERFORMANCE

This is more of the die-hard self-development stuff that you see in performance/success-based books. Trying to get the fire in your belly going and planning your next steps.

This book has touched on several topics and key areas throughout, which I attribute to personal development.

The whole area is a minefield and this book could go on for the rest of my eternity. We should always be working on ourselves and there will always be areas which we can improve.

I wanted to discuss the following points as I feel they cover the core basic skills to help with improving your 'performance' and getting your life heading in a direction you wish it to go. This is an area I am really passionate about and it is where I see my future heading with helping others. It is about getting the fire in your belly going a little.

Tony Robbins labels the second pillar of an 'extraordinary life' as the science of achievement. This is what most are quite obsessed with, are fully aware of, and often chase. It means taking what you envision and making it real. He describes it as a science. There is a science to building wealth; if you follow the rules, you will build it. There is a science to having energy in the human body; if you follow the rules, you will have it.

I wanted to pull out what I believe to be the most relevant content related to performance and condense it to this section.

We have mentioned that nobody is going to change your life for you and it is solely you who must do this. To do this, we must take action!

LIFE BALANCE/GOAL SETTING

I wanted to first offer some of my advice concerning goal setting. Goal setting can apply to literally any area of our lives. Some people are very much in the habit of goal setting, whereas others may never set goals.

In our hectic lives, it can sometimes be difficult to work out what goals to set and where we want to improve. Similarly, we can become so focused on certain areas that we start to neglect others.

I wanted to start with what I believe to be one of the best methods for realising where you wish to improve in your life and a tool I often revisit to assess where I am managing in my life.

This tool is one that helps to find balance and is a tool used by many life coaches.

It is known as the 'life wheel' (or balance wheel), and it allows you to rate your satisfaction in different areas of your life. This then gives you an overview and can help you realise where you need to start making changes and what areas need attention. It was said to be first developed by Paul J. Meyer in 1960.

The original wheel of life looked something like this:

- Family and **Home**
- Financial and **Career**
- Spiritual and **Ethical**
- Mental and **Education**
- Social and **Cultural**
- Physical and **Health**

This is good guidance to follow. For my wheel of life, I add extra topics such as self-development. In addition to this, I may add in a specific topic I am working on, for example, 'writing my book'. If I then mark it as an area that is not doing as well as it should be, I create some basic action points to change this. This should be specific to you.

The great part of the life balance worksheet is that it will give you a great insight into your life as a whole. This means that you can immediately set about making any necessary changes.

Without the right balance, we can feel discontent and unhappy. A good life will leave us feeling creative, happy and fulfilled, so it should be completed regularly and taken seriously.

Journal —Wheel of life

Below is a blank wheel of life:

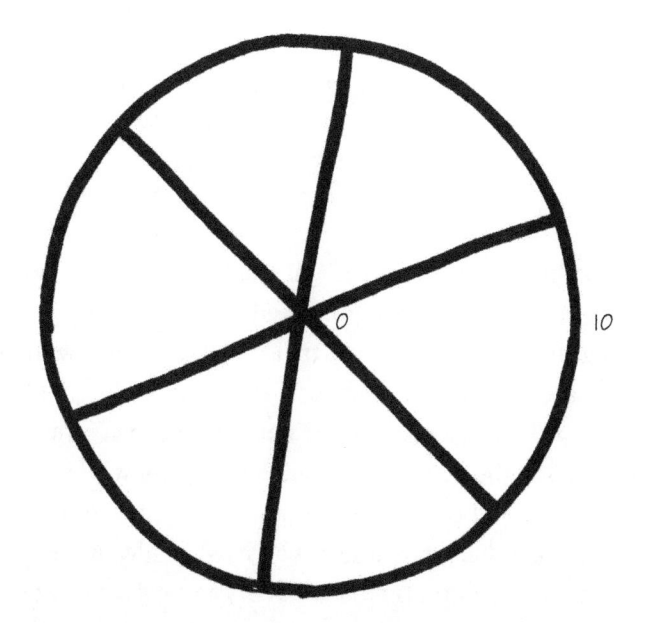

Instructions:
- Name the categories so that it is meaningful for you.
- The centre of the wheel represents 0 – and the outer is 10.
- Mark on your circle where you feel your life currently sits (0 being poor and 10 being great).
- Start taking action to change this.

An important point to remember is that complete balance is rarely achieved for long periods. This is because life shifts and changes often; the goal is not to achieve a full life balance, but the idea is to ensure you are moving towards it rather than away from it. Completing the wheel of life allows you to see where you need improvement visually, then you can start taking action to achieve this.

Setting goals continued

> "If you want to be happy, set a goal that commands your thoughts, liberates your energy and inspires your hopes."
> Andrew Carnegie

I cannot stress enough that if you want to achieve things in life you need to set goals. You need to know where you're heading. If you set off driving to a new destination without a roadmap, you will likely get lost. The same applies in life. I was 'lost', as I didn't know where I wanted to go in life. Yes, this was down to other reasons too, but I did not know what I was aiming for. Now, I consistently set goals to aim for. You might not always get there, but at least you have an idea where you are going. The same applies for everybody; if you want to know where to head to in your life, you have to set some fucking goals!

I don't want to overcomplicate this area, so I will start with a basic task. I set three main goals for this year.

- Inspire others (start a blog, podcast and begin speaking publicly).

- Complete a book to positively serve others.
- Save £5,000 by the end of the year.

The reason I am telling you this is so that you can see what I am working towards. I see these goals every single day and I can then ask myself. Am I working towards my goals today? What am I going to do today to work towards my goals?

It gives me something to work towards.

I want you to now write three of your most important goals:

- _____
- _____
- _____

Journal

Using the below space, I want you to complete the following for your 'most important goal' from the above list as it will help to break your goal down further. If you do not have any goals yet stop and give some time to thinking about what you want to achieve as I cannot stress this the importance of this enough.

Goal statement:

_____
_____
_____
_____
_____

How will this goal benefit me personally?

What steps do I need to take to achieve this goal?

Who can help me achieve this goal?

What obstacles are there? What solutions are there?

I will have this goal completed by:

This is just a basic template, but it gets you thinking about your goals. Another method I like to apply is to work backwards. Once you have envisioned your 'overall goal', start making a note of the steps that you need to take to achieve this goal, going right back to the very first actionable step you can take. At first a goal might seem huge and unattainable, but by breaking it down into smaller steps, it starts to help you see what needs to be achieved. I once seen this referred to as 'chunking', and it is taking one big goal and breaking it into bitesize chunks.

Your goal might be to lose two stone. Break this down further into smaller goals, such as increasing your physical activity or reducing your calorie intake, and it is going to start to feel more achievable. You can break the goals down further, and I would encourage this; list weekly or even daily tasks/goals which are going to contribute to you achieving the bigger longer-term goal.

CREATE A VISION BOARD/PAGE

Another *huge* motivating factor can be to create a vision board. Having something 'visual' to look at daily can provide massive motivation towards striving for goals. You can make this as big as you want. I have a painted chalkboard paint in my study room (my partner thinks I am crazy!). Get a big whiteboard. Write your goals on this in big bold letters. How are you going to get there? Why are you doing what you do? Place inspiring quotes on there. Even place pictures of the things you desire in your life. Put up pictures of things you wish to try, places you want to go. Start making action points of the changes you're going to make. There is a whole science to all of this and this book won't do it justice. There are other areas such as 'visualising' your goals, but this is just a snapshot of areas here. A vision board can help you be creative, as well as give you focus. It makes your dreams clear and it makes you more determined; having something to aim for is going to serve you well. It can be related to any area of your life.

Journal

Below is a hypothetical vision board. This can be used as a draft and you can transfer this to a neater piece of paper or larger area. I also want you to create one of these in your journal that you carry with you daily. This is just a draft example, but with your full versions try and spend some real time making them applicable to you.

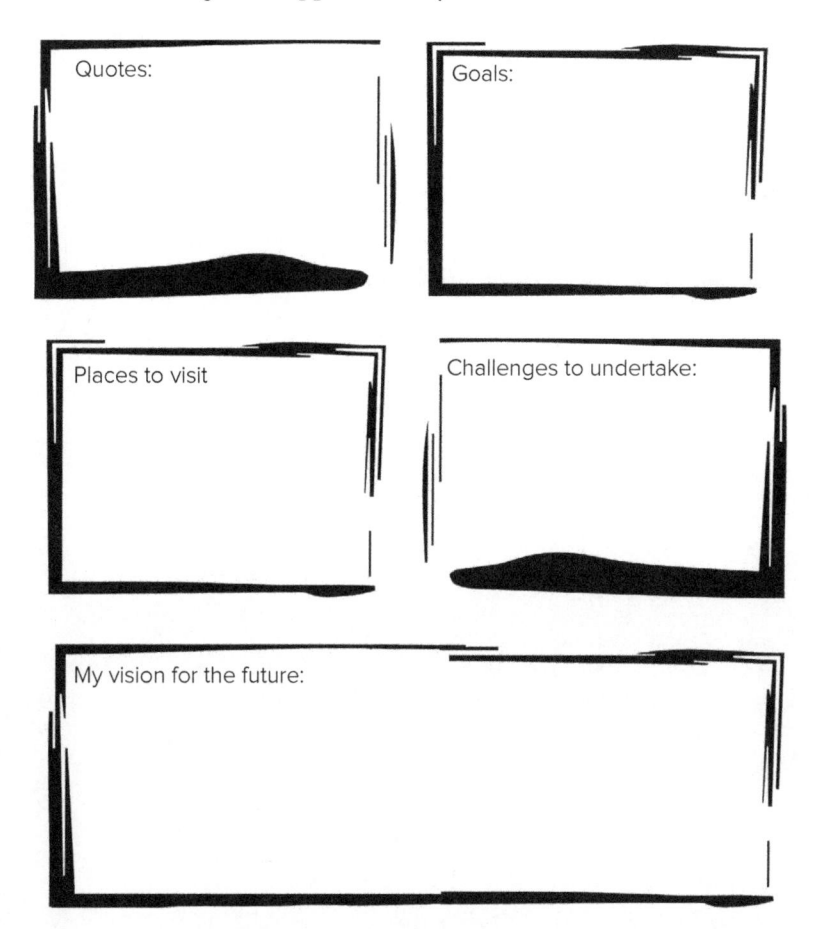

Quotes:

Goals:

Places to visit

Challenges to undertake:

My vision for the future:

Why do you want to achieve this?

Positive affirmations:

TAKE ACTION

Once we have set the goals and made the vision board, we must take action. Lots of action. This book did not write itself. These goals won't just start coming true. I cannot stress this enough.

I am learning now that a little action is much better than doing nothing at all.

> "A goal without an action plan is a daydream."
> Nathaniel Branden

I feel as if I have heard this quote a thousand times from a thousand people. However, it bears truth. In certain parts of my life, I have failed with this concept, I have thought I have wanted something and then failed to take steps to complete it. I have nobody else to blame but myself.

Unless we take action, then we will get nowhere. As much as I have loved writing this book, there have been occasions when I could have chosen to put it down and focused my attention on something else. I had to dedicate a lot of time to it. This is my first ever book – it won't happen as naturally for me as others; it required a lot of focus and dedication.

I am a big fan of the law of attraction and vision boards and visualisation, etc., but without action, it is pointless. It is like imagining your favourite dessert and then just expecting it to appear in your mouth. Yes, this would be amazing, but it isn't going to happen.

Mel Robbins suggests that it doesn't matter how big the goal is; it is simply about taking small, actionable, achievable goals. She suggests we build a house by firstly laying the foundations. Therefore, to achieve our goals, we must take it 'one brick at a time'. She uses the phrase 'brick by brick to make it stick', and it is about taking small actions daily to achieve your goal.

I attended a seminar by Steven Green on Mindset; he kept saying that, "Life rewards action-takers." He believes success is a choice and our actions determine every result; we all have the ability to choose success, but taking action is a must.

In regard to 'choosing success', a lot of my problems stemmed from feeling like a failure; to put it another way, 'success' was always something I felt I lacked. However, my favourite definition of success is that of Earl Nightingale:

> "Success is the progressive realization of a worthy ideal."

Your 'worthy ideal' being your personal goals and dreams. 'Success', therefore, is about consistently working towards this idea, this predetermined goal, whatever that is to you. However, you need something to work towards! Thankfully,

I am establishing these goals now and working towards them consistently; you must do so too.

This is why having goals is so important; they give us focus, meaning and purpose, and the biggest thing you can do to make positive changes in your life is to take consistent action, no matter how big or how small.

In regard to all the concepts I have discussed in this book and will continue to discuss, this is just theory at present; it's only when we take action on them that we will see results.

CREATING HABITS

How do we achieve goals? Well, we need to start changing our habits.

The truth is, we do not have to make sudden catastrophic changes and completely change our life (although some will instantly); we just have to start taking small action now.

Developing habits = small changes daily.

In the book *Atomic Habits* by James Clear, he wrote that the truth is, we only have to look to become one per cent better each day. I mentioned this at the start of the book.

You have probably heard this old, cliché saying:

"My only goal is to be better than I was yesterday."

However, it is so true. It is about making small steps and small steps only within the twenty-four hours we have each day.

Although we may not consciously see them, implementing small changes every day makes a difference.

If we worked out for twenty minutes a day, we wouldn't see the results immediately after the first session, but over time, we would start to see the changes. Likewise, if we eat pizza every day, we wouldn't immediately see the changes, but over time, we would gain weight.

In *The Compound Effect* by Dan Hardy, he talks about how long-term success stems from consistent actions hammered out daily. We live in a world where we want everything right now, with instant gratification, for success to just immediately happen (I would be lying if I hadn't been sold by some millionaire-maker Facebook ad at one point, and we see it everywhere with the latest diet fads and so forth), but let's be realistic – it doesn't work like that. It takes small actions repeated over time and we should enjoy the process of improving yourself. I am repeating this over and over because it also serves as a reminder to me. I am impatient at times and expect instant results. It simply does not work like that.

In *Atomic Habits*, the author also talks about making habits enjoyable. If we don't like working out, change it – watch something you do enjoy whilst doing the workout, mix it up a bit. We can literally stick an exercise bike in front of the TV; things can be adapted easily if you just think outside the box.

In the local gym I use they have YouTube available on the treadmills – how awesome is this? I am not a huge fan of running, I will be honest, but I know it is critical to my fitness, so I get it done. I now use my time running to watch Thai boxing fights on videos or listen to self-development audiotapes and this, to me, serves as a slight distraction to watching the timer and praying I am almost done. I also get to learn new knowledge simultaneously, which is a bonus. Stick on an audiotape and go for a walk (use a motivating one). You can utilise your time very well whilst also making a number of positive changes.

MORNING ROUTINES

One of the best ways to create habits is to create a routine.

> *"If you win the morning... you win the day."*
> Tim Ferris

This is not going to be a lecture on how you must be up at 4am in order to succeed.

However, morning routines can have a massive impact on, firstly, your mental wellbeing, but also on making sure that you can complete necessary tasks. I aim to get up at 6.30am. This is achievable for me. I like my sleep too! And it is so important to our health. Getting up early allows me to get shit done! It helps you to start the day right.

I start official work at 8.30am. If I am up by 6.30am, I can practise morning gratitude, go to the gym, have a stable breakfast, listen to an audiotape or read something positive, meditate or stretch, which means by the time I arrive to work I feel great already – I am fully energised and ready to go instead of dragging my feet to get there.

Sometimes I have been up earlier and managed to catch the sunrise at a local walking sight, and this immediately fills me with positive energy and an appreciation for life.

This is what works for me. However, your morning routine can be completely individual to you. You can start by trying to get up half an hour earlier. This can allow you to perhaps get some chores done that would normally need to wait till after work or do other activities, which then frees up more time later in the day. Then try to increase this to an hour.

It may be that it is not for you, but give it a go and see if it makes a difference. If you don't do it currently, just imagine what an extra half an hour could bring to your day?

Increased organisation and productivity, reduced stress, instilling good habits – the list is endless.

Journal

Create a morning routine

I now want to help you create a positive morning routine. Follow the below guidance of mine as an example, but make it specific to you. Write down some ideas of what you would like to get done and create a routine. Stick it somewhere you can see it daily (like your notebook), then start setting your alarm that little bit earlier and start your day right.

Here is an example of mine:

THE BOOK THAT BECAME MY COUNSELLOR

	Monday	Tuesday	Wednesday	Thursday	Friday	Saturday	Sunday
Gratitude							
Quote of the day							
Healthy Juice/ breakfast							
Workout							
Recite goals							

MORNING ROUTINES

Your morning routine:

Monday					
Tuesday					
Wednesday					
Thursday					
Friday					
Saturday					
Sunday					

Another bit of advice for your morning routine would be to set intentions for the day – what is it that you must get complete today in order to move further forward. This allows you to start the day off with a very healthy mindset. I like to write my 'daily wins' (what's important now), and this is three things that I need to get done that day to bring me closer to my goals. It helps keep me focused and wasting less time doing pointless tasks (which we have probably all been guilty of at some stage).

STOP LIVING IN FEAR

Given we have a section about achieving goals, I think it also makes sense to talk about the concept of fear as well, because this can hold us back significantly.

> "Fear is the most subtle and destructive of all human diseases; fear kills dreams and hope."
> Les Brown

The concept of 'fear' again could have a whole book written on it. It is something that every single one of us has been beaten by at some point in our lives.

However, the truth is that we are only actually born with two fears – the fear of falling and the fear of loud noises.

Any other fears you experience have been acquired throughout your life and are often caused by certain events and situations that have marked your mind and emotions in a way that makes you feel scared, and that's when our body responds with the 'fight or flight' response.

Apparently, though…

> *"The only thing we should fear is fear itself!"*
> Franklin. D. Roosevelt

For so many people, the fear of failure is a huge barrier that can overwhelm their will to try anything new. In *'13 things mentally strong people don't do'*, Amy Morin also says we so often tend to think that success just falls from the sky. However, success often only comes after a long road of failure. Mentally strong people know how to persevere and treat their failures as stepping stones to something greater. The key to overcoming the fear of failure lies in self-compassion and changing the way you think about failure.

Do not fear failure because you would be more pissed off by regret in your later years. In hindsight, if this book seriously fails… should I be really disheartened? There is nothing majorly lost by trying. It just means sucking it up and trying again.

To put it into context, Les Brown, one of my favourite motivational speakers, says that the graveyard is the place where some of the biggest hopes, ideas, dreams and not dared intentions are left. He says imagine being on your deathbed and seeing the ghosts of your potential and knowing you hadn't even tried. Yet so many of us are restricted because of a number of things we have discussed in this book. We lack belief, we fear other people's opinion or we have fears of what could go wrong. If you have goals and ambitions, don't let this be you.

Some people that have gone on to achieve huge success had to experience various failures along the way.

- Twelve publishing houses rejected JK Rowling's *Harry Potter* manuscript before Bloomsbury finally took her on. Well, we all know how that ended up!
- Thomas Edison made one thousand unsuccessful attempts at inventing the light bulb. Apparently when asked, "How did it feel to fail one thousand times?", he replied, "I didn't fail one thousand times. The light bulb was an invention with one thousand steps." Now how is that for inspiration?
- Then take Sir James Dyson – he apparently went through 5,126 failed prototypes over the course of fifteen years before creating the eponymous best-selling bagless vacuum cleaner that led to his net worth going into the billions. That is persistence on a vision and purpose for yourself.

All these people overcame what could be seen as failure and went on to succeed in a huge way. They may have been scared to pick themselves back up again and keep persevering, but they did it, and look what they achieved. You need to use fear as a motivating tool, turning the fear of not doing something into the fear or regretting that decision later. As this book approached publication, there were times I got scared, but I turned that fear around by thinking about how I would feel if I hadn't at least given it a go. I felt I had to do it for myself and to help others. Again, what do you have to lose?

To add to this, the first ten plus publishers rejected this manuscript, and I never just threw it in the bin. I managed a 'part publishing' deal, which means I still had to invest myself. However, the money was irrelevant; it was something I was so determined to do. I still have no idea how it will fare.

We fetishize success and are taught from a young age to fear failure. Life is ruled by achieving exam results and performing on tests like it's the end of the world. In my opinion, this is a load of bollocks. Many people in life have not achieved what they have without failure, so we should not fear it.

I get it, though; this takes work. I am in no way completely fearless when it comes to trying new things. I am not fearless in all situations. I am just trying to learn to be a bit braver.

BREAK OUT OF YOUR COMFORT ZONE

"Your comfort zone is a beautiful place, but nothing ever grows there."

Unknown

Following on from the above nicely, in order to be braver, we have to leave what is often described as our 'comfort zone'.

Stepping out of your 'comfort zone' is something that we often hear we need to do; I think it's in every self-development book ever produced (I told you I wasn't reinventing the wheel!) backed up by countless motivating quotes.

In some of the literature, your 'comfort zone' is described as a feeling of being 'safe and in control', so I will start by saying… it is nice to feel comfortable in our daily lives, whether this is in business or life. Leaving your comfort zone, on the other hand, can initiate that internal dialogue of what could go wrong, how we could be judged and countless other feelings of 'discomfort'. (Which fundamentally stem from fear, as described above.)

So why are we constantly told to leave it? We would not purposely choose to buy an uncomfortable bed or sofa, or sit in uncomfortable clothes, so why should we choose to feel uncomfortable in our life pursuits? Well, the truth is, we do not have to! I would argue that in most cases, nobody is holding a gun to your head to make you do anything! And if you do not want to leave your comfort zone… Well, then don't!

But… if you do want to grow on a personal level, then we must be prepared to feel uncomfortable. Why? Because if we are feeling uncomfortable about a decision or action we must do, it is probably because it is going to test us in some way. This is a good thing! It is probably going to help us improve our skills.

There are too many examples to list. However, by leaving your comfort zone it allows you to chase your dreams, to explore new things (hobbies and interests), to become the best version of you (in whatever industry), as well as achieving many more positive outcomes.

It will feel scary. As stated above, I still have moments where I get fearful of doing new things. However, I am trying to get used to the feeling of 'getting comfortable with the uncomfortable', as I know it is so important for my personal growth. I now try to set myself at least one weekly 'comfort zone breaker' within my journal, and I would challenge you to do the same.

Your comfort zone is only trying to protect you from your fears, but on the other side of it could be the person you want to be (with a new career as a top salesperson, a new hobby... so many possibilities).

This is the thing as well: once you have done something, it will get easier, and then we can look to set further challenges. I am still a way off where I want to be, but I have a growth mindset, and I am always looking to improve; we should always be looking to progress. But to do so we must leave that comfort zone.

To end on a nice quote and action point:

> "You can only grow if you are willing to feel awkward and uncomfortable when you try something new."
>
> Brian Tracey

Journal: Fear and Comfort Zones

Please use the below area to make any notes on the above sections. As well as this, consider the following questions:

What is the one thing you are going to do today, this week, to take you outside of your comfort zone?

What would be the benefits to you stepping outside your comfort zone?

What if you knew you could not fail? List five things you would do right now if you knew you could not fail.

Identify your fears. What is it that is stopping you from taking action?

BREAK OUT OF YOUR COMFORT ZONE

Why should I leave my comfort zone? What will happen if I decide to make that step?

___

Also consider things such as, does this idea excite me? Will I feel regret if I never go for it? Will taking action help me move forward?

___

Answer them honestly; you don't have to say yes – there isn't a correct answer – but if something is holding you back, at least you can identify it. This will then give you areas to work on.

Notes:

AVOID PERFECTIONISM AND LIMIT DISTRACTIONS

In order to achieve our goals and to make progress, we also must avoid perfectionism. I learned during this process how much it was holding me back. When it came to be nearing the end of this book, I was spending so much time editing, reshuffling paragraphs, adding them, removing them, rewording them and trying to make it sound perfect. It was becoming a source of stress for me. My enjoyment started to diminish. Perfectionism can become toxic, so don't be so hard on yourself to get everything perfect; take action consistently, and you will move closer to your goals, rather than trying to get everything absolutely right every time. Striving for progress and not perfection is an excellent way to approach all your goals in life.

Finally, avoid distractions. This is a productivity killer. I have been guilty of it myself. I would have my phone on the table as I was writing; I would become distracted and stop. When I removed the phone from the equation, my productivity went up tenfold. If you have bad habits and you know what distracts you, then do your best to remove them. I have a friend in business who deletes his social media apps during the week. This is because he recognises it holds him back, so when he removes it from the equation, his productivity goes up.

SUMMARY

In order to really achieve our goals in life, the most important thing we must do is take action. We can dream all we want, but without going out and taking action, we will never move forwards. That is the simple formula. Remember, life rewards action-takers. There is a guy I know called Paul Million (a real successful property entrepreneur who has an awesome mindset) – he once said to me, "Either shit on the pot or get off it," and this was a response to me procrastinating about an idea for such a long time. Stewing over the idea wasn't taking me forward in any way.

Little wins each day add up to longer-term success. Look at your goals daily to remind yourself of them. *Carry a goal card* with you so each time you open it, you're reminded of your goals and it motivates you to take action. Stick it as your phone background, so you see it every time you open your phone. Have them in your journal. Put them fucking anywhere that is going to remind you of them! Reassess them regularly; are you making progress?

My best advice for productivity would be to plan

accordingly (plan your week and also plan your day). Spend some time on a Sunday evening planning for the week ahead. I sometimes appreciate things come up and schedules change, but it gives you a general guideline to follow. Make a list of actions you are going to take that week and make yourself accountable for what you achieve.

In terms of general living, I have a 'habit tracker' in my journal, which I fill in daily. This includes things such as 'workout', 'morning juice', 'listen to an audiobook'. This has allowed me to literally develop healthier habits daily, which helps me live a healthier life.

If you feel you won't make yourself accountable, ask a friend to help you out and report to them weekly; you can then review whether you are carrying out what you said you were going to.

Finally... **most importantly...**

CARRY A JOURNAL

To re-emphasise this point again. Carry a journal with you at all times. A pocket diary or anything. Use it to create ideas, to write down inspiring stuff, to plan your day, to write down your gratitude, to write down your wins, to write down something positive your children or partner did. To write the best version of yourself, to write your goals, have a mini vision board, check your morning routine. Plan your week. Log your habits. Have it on you permanently and use it to push you towards success and fulfilment. These are sometimes referred to as 'performance planners' and are sold as these; they are great. For me it is my personal journal, adapted to me, my very own counsellor where I can still write my thoughts and feelings as well as ideas and goals. There was no way I was doing this stuff when I was at my lowest; again, this stuff has changed my life, and I am just getting started.

I hope by this stage in the book, you have now purchased your own personal journal.

GENERAL LIFE ADVICE

As this book is discussing wellbeing, I wanted to give some of my 'everyday life' tips that I try to incorporate to make sure that I get to enjoy life and I don't just watch it pass by me.

Below are some things I think you can be doing to help you to be generally happier in life and some actionable advice.

PLAY MORE...
engage in hobbies... have fun... or just do something you enjoy!

"The opposite of play is not work, it's depression."
Brian Sutton Smith

I feel one of the best ways to boost positive emotions is to have some fun, to enjoy yourself. It seems simple when I say it, but so many of us just don't do it.

Think about it as children; we had so much fucking fun, didn't we? I loved it! I was out and about kicking a football and then climbing trees until it went dark. Then as adults, we get so serious. Yes, life gets more serious; we enter the 'real' world and we have to work and pay bills, etc., but we shouldn't stop having fun.

I have heard it once described as 'the medicine of play'.

> "Play keeps us vital and alive. It gives us an enthusiasm for life that is irreplaceable. Without it, life just doesn't taste good."
> Lucia Capacchione

Play is healthy and fun. It releases endorphins, improves brain function and even promotes creativity. Einstein once said, "Play is the highest form of research." So it is also crucial for our personal development.

And by fun, I don't just mean going to the pub (yes, that can be fun too) but getting out and doing things (see below).

Journal A list of hobbies – get out and have fun

I am going to do a very basic exercise here by copying one that I have done previously for myself. What I am about to do is not a ground-breaking exercise. It is just one I have found to work for me.

So many people are living unfulfilled lives. So many people are living lives that is missing the essence of fun and play. We evaluate finances, careers, relationships, etc., but do we ever stop to evaluate if we're having enough fun and enjoying life? Go back and add it to your wheel of life at this stage if you need to!

Make a list of activities that do not cost a great deal of money, and go and do them.

It can be things such as a picnic in the park. Cooking as a family. Or be spontaneous and make a list of activities you have not done in a while. Perhaps list some completely new ones on there.

I made one before, and it was called my 'not forgetting to live' checklist. The reason being, so many of us get so caught up in doing other things that we forget to live now. I have been guilty of this too, however life is about enjoying it. We are all creatures of habit too, so try and mix it up a little bit and try something new and exciting.

Go on Google and search for a list of things to do in your area. You may find some things that you never knew existed.

'Not forgetting to live' checklist

I want you to try and list at least twelve fun activities that you feel you would be able to do over the next month; regardless of how busy your schedule is, find the time to do it. It will be a great mood booster.

1.
2.
3.
4.
5.
6.
7.
8.
9.
10.
11.
12.

A simple way to be happier is to do more things that make you happy. This doesn't have to be monthly; it can be weekly or even daily. Make a list of things that make you happy and see how many of them you can fit into your schedule.

GET OUTDOORS

I have found personally one of my greatest healers and the biggest benchmarks for my own self-development has been to get outdoors.

The idea for me is that being outdoors in nature allows me to feel connected to something greater than myself. It's got me into a transcendent state. It has really helped me to stop and think and really ask a lot of questions surrounding life and meaning and who I am. I suppose, reflecting on it, it is probably the spiritual side of my personal development, which hasn't really been mentioned in this book, but it is something I find myself starting to work on. It has also really helped with my journaling and therefore It has been crucial to my self-development. This is something that many years ago I would never have envisioned myself doing or certainly writing about; it would have challenged my masculine ego too much. "Fucking hell, Joe, that's deep." I imagine would be the response if this was discussed in the pub.

In her book *The Power of Meaning*, Emily Smith refers to transcendence as the fourth pillar of meaning. When you're in a transcendent state of mind, the barriers between yourself and the wider world dissolve. She refers to the psychologist David Yaden, who believes that in a transcendent state, a person feels connected to everything around them. It is at this moment that a person loses any sense of anxiety, feels complete peace and optimal wellbeing, and derives meaning in life. This is a little bit 'deeper' than you might expect, but this is the feeling I get.

The complete quietness in nature allows me to relax completely. The sound of the natural water flowing is the complete opposite of the huge trucks that pass by my house on the main road daily. As well as this, it is simply good fun, and it makes me happy.

I am not saying that going outdoors is your answer, as this is entirely subjective to me. However, I would certainly give it a try. It has worked so many wonders for me that I just cannot write this book without mentioning it.

PUT DOWN YOUR FUCKING PHONE
(well, at least when not required) and look after your own battery life

Perhaps a controversial bit of advice, but I do think another thing that we do currently is spend too much time on our phones.

Some people say our phones are the best things that were ever invented, and in some respects, I wholeheartedly agree. They can be unbelievable for business; they can be unbelievable for self-development with the amazing apps as well as audiobooks, etc. They also connect the world. They are fucking brilliant, put simply, and have advanced so much even in my lifetime.

However, at the same time, don't allow it to make you distant from the people who are directly in front of you, as you don't know how much time you have with these people. They can affect your relationships with loved ones, as you spend less time talking and more time scrolling.

Similarly, there is nothing more frustrating than being at a social gathering with friends and noticing every single one of them sat staring at their screens. I have been guilty of this myself in the past (I still can be may I add, I am not preaching to you I am simply making suggestions), but I do try making a conscious effort to hide my phone away when it is not really needed. When we think about it, it is just rude more than anything, and to me personally, it says, what I am saying to you is not really that important.

They also can be a complete waste of time. I would often find myself wasting hours and hours scrolling through Facebook, Instagram and other social media platforms. (Again, I still sometimes waste time now, although I try to be more conscious of it.) For me, it became so habitual that I wouldn't stop to take the world in and truly appreciate the things that made me happy. Not only that, I was also wasting hours and hours looking at other people's shit when I could be better spending the time working on myself.

My partner and I have tried to make a habit of banning phones from the dinner table, and when I go out for tea with my family, I will leave my phone in the car. How many times must we have missed opportunities to speak with people in front of us, because we were so busy caught up looking at what other people were doing with their day through our phones?

So, I am not saying don't ever use your phone, but try to use it more intelligently. You can always check Facebook once you finish your family meal. Again, to re-emphasise, platforms such as Facebook and Instagram can be inspiring for new ideas, but my advice would be to limit your time on them. Try not to spend a third of your day scrolling through unnecessary nonsense. Try to truly take moments in instead of missing everything because of your phone.

If you want to think of your mobile phone as a necessity, use it as a life metaphor:

> "You wouldn't let your phone battery die, so don't let it happen to you either; self-care is a priority, not a luxury."
>
> Unknown

Think about it – the frustration people have when their phone battery dies and the anxiety it causes. You have to have the same focus on not letting your mental battery die, work on it, charge your wellbeing up.

Likewise, don't let your relationships die because of your phone. We are closer than ever as humans, but phones are also allowing us to be so distant from each other at the same time. So be conscious and try to put your phone down for a short period.

Also change the reality of the content you follow. By following more motivating/positive content groups on Facebook, I was finding that when I did look at my news feed, there was much more encouraging content to follow. To me personally, this is so much more inspiring than seeing what someone had for breakfast. Give it a try.

SPEND TIME WITH LOVED ONES
make the call if you have to

I have lost count of the number of times I have heard people moaning 'X' does not get in touch anymore. This is why I felt it's a point I had to make. However, the truth is, we can always reach out. If there is someone whom you miss or wish to connect with, we have the tools to reach out (the mobile phone being a positive example now). Yet so many of us fail to do so because we sit there angry, feeling like they should reach out to us first. However, that close friend could be sitting there, thinking the same thing. Alternatively, they might just have something going on where they cannot pluck up the courage to reach out. They could have completely changed as a person and you will then realise you no longer want to have them in your life. The truth is, you don't know. However, do not allow the unknown and do not look back with regret because you failed to reach out to someone. Make the call, go and see your relative, spend time with those you love. Life is too short.

GET SOCIAL

We, as humans, are social beings. Joining a community is a great way to help you with whatever your quest may be. For example, if you want to lose weight, give up alcohol or drugs, you have an increased chance of doing so by joining groups. In business, it is stressed that your network is fundamental to your development. I discussed the importance of your physical environment on your personal development earlier on in the book.

According to psychologist Henry Cloud, this is because positivity is contagious. We are more likely to succeed when part of a community due to four key reasons: first, we can learn from other group members; second, competition within the group helps our performance; third, we are held accountable to the community; and fourth, we motivate and encourage each other.

Another thing that we can never get enough of is connectedness, i.e. our connections to and communication with others. In fact, across many books I have read, several studies have demonstrated that the happiest people are those who spend the most time socialising. So even if you're not spending time in a focused group, make sure you get out with friends regularly!

I **love** socialising.

SLOW DOWN

This is rich coming from me. I have spent my days running around like a headless chicken at times, totally chaotic.

Also, in the 'performance' part, we talked about goal setting and morning routines and productivity. I get it…how can you slow down and do this?

Too often, we are too stressed to enjoy life, but a little slowness can go a long way in changing that.

We forget to have fun (as already highlighted). We forget to relax. We are often left with such little time we are petrified to lose a second. I have literally created anxiety about 'time' on so many occasions.

In the book *The Ruthless Elimination of Hurry* by John Comer, he calls it the 'hurry disease'. Modern life is so fast-paced, it has become so normal to rush from task to task, appointment to appointment, even eating dinner, so that we don't even notice we do it; our lives could be different. It is a genuine threat to our wellbeing, as trying to do everything and be everywhere is unrealistic and is making us exhausted.

It's true; everything says we need to keep working and

keep working and keep working. He even says if we had 'more time', it wouldn't make us less busy, it would just mean that we would have more time to be busy.

We don't often give ourselves time to think; social media means we're never alone with our thoughts. A study featured in *Business Insider* reported that the average iPhone user touches their phone no less than 2,617 times per day! (This has already highlighted as an issue.) Perhaps if we did just stop for a second, we might have some of our best ideas.

We used to get moments away from our thoughts, moments which he calls 'quiet contemplation' – waiting in line, staring out the window of buses, solitude which we would now call boredom – but it has all become extinct.

Comer suggests we make sure to create time for silence and solitude. This is why I love camping and the outdoors! It allows me to shut off from the fast-paced world.

However, you don't need this to get some time alone. He suggests getting up an hour earlier and enjoying a cup of coffee in your favourite chair. Get off the bus earlier and have a leisurely stroll to work, taking everything in.

We live in a consuming world, needing more and more, but I think to find some happiness, we sometimes have to slow down.

TRY TO 'SWITCH OFF'
relax, meditate or just take a long breath!

In order to slow down, we also must find ways in which we can calm ourselves down daily, which will also aid our mental wellbeing.

There are a few ways I find myself able to do this. Mindfulness (flick back to the task earlier) or a meditation-based exercise. Any breathing exercises. They don't have to be long-winded. Just stop and try to find five minutes. Do some more research on this.

Another method is a simple relaxation technique using calming music. I used this initially as a sleeping aid! Constant thoughts were buzzing through my head; I felt myself having to make to-do lists late at night (I have since curbed this with better planning). Try listening to some soothing music while you have some time to relax.

Take a bath. Read a book (hopefully this one). Or find some time to relax in whatever way works for you.

As much as I love being focused and productive, and I do love socialising, we need to make sure we are putting the time aside to focus on ourselves.

Some 'me time' is so important to our wellbeing too.

PHILOSOPHICAL GUIDANCE

Something a little bit more 'philosophical', or touching on a few points that get you thinking about your approach to life.

CHANGE YOUR PERCEPTION OF LIFE ITSELF

> "If you want to, you can find a million reasons to hate life and be angry at the world. Or, if you want to, you could find a million reasons to love life and be happy. Choose wisely."
>
> Cari Welsh

Easier said than done? Let's be true to ourselves: the world is full of challenges and suffering, but this isn't cause for despair. In *12 Rules for Life* by Jordan Peterson, he insists we must make the best out of even the smallest of joys that life offers. By doing so, you will embrace life more and appreciate the very good things that comes your way. It will also help you through the tough times, even when they are prolonged.

Albert Einstein once said the most fundamental and major decision you must make in life is whether you live in a friendly or hostile universe.

The world can often be cruel, and we are always faced

with challenges. However, if we look to find a cruel world, that is exactly what we will find. As Tony Robbins famously says, "Seek and you shall find."

This is where our RAS comes in. Our reticular activating system. This is known as the brains 'filter' system. Our brain takes in so much information at any one second but can only process so much at one time. So, it lets through information that it feels is important: what you are focusing on, thinking about or are aware of. Think about when we get a new car; we suddenly start seeing that same car everywhere. Those same model and same colour cars have always been there; it is only now that we start taking note of them. Therefore, it is important that we are careful about what we focus on.

If we say to ourselves that 'we are a failure' (using my example), our brain will seek out information that matches this story we have created for ourselves. The more we see, the stronger the belief grows that it is true. On the flip side, we need to use it to our advantage: set your RAS to look for the positives. This is where positive self-belief comes in. Start telling yourself, you are great, you are capable of what you wish to achieve. If you are looking to achieve a goal, set your RAS to work for you, not against you.

Going back to the perception point, I once heard a YouTube video that said if you were to go on Google and search 'how bad things happen to good people', you would instantly get about half a million responses that matched what you were searching for.

Likewise, if you googled 'how good things happen to good people', you would also get a huge number of responses that matched this perception.

With Google, you can find answers for anything, which you choose to believe in, no matter what it is.

The same goes for life; start looking for the good in things and you will start to notice them more, thus helping you feel more positive.

LIFE IS AN EXPERIMENT

> "All life is an experiment;
> the more experiments you make, the better."
>
> Ralph Waldo Emmerson

Another positive, and what I believe to be a great philosophical approach to life, is to look at it as an experiment.

From a personal perspective, I suffered mentally because I expected to have my life worked out the moment I left school. This wasn't the case. It doesn't need to be either! I wish they would send out this message more in schools.

I always looked at it with an entirely negative perspective, whereas I can reflect differently now.

People do try different things, and not everything goes as planned. We won't always get life right, but we shouldn't berate ourselves for this. It is the things we do not try that people should fear more. We will also hopefully learn more from those moments that perhaps didn't work out. This is critical to our self-development.

Regarding this book, I got to a point where I was

procrastinating so much, trying to get it perfect. Questioning every single detail. Will it work? Won't it? Is the structure right, etc.? Will it be a success? Will it flop? I don't know the outcome of this; I really don't. This is my first time writing one! I may as well experiment and just go with it. If it flops, I will get some shit Amazon reviews (or none at all) and then life goes on. Alternatively, it could do well. We never seem to question what could go right, as we are too busy focusing on what could go wrong. It is the default mode in us as humans; again I hold my hands up to this more than once. However, next time you find yourself creating every scenario in your head about what might go wrong, stop for a second and think, What happens if this all works out? Then what?

I was once told that the only guarantee in life is dying, which is a little bit morbid, I get it; however, things seem a little bit less trivial when you consider this.

If you are stuck on whether to pursue something through fear, or whatever other reason, ask yourself, what is the worst that could happen?

In the time we do have here, our happiness and personal wellbeing should always come before absolutely everything. We must try and make the most of it. Life is for living and enjoying, so try new hobbies. Try new things. Experiment with life!

IF ALL ELSE FAILS...
use the 'fuck-it bucket' approach

Perhaps not one of life's most typical philosophical approaches, but something I love nonetheless.

As much as I am a fan of this phrase, it is not my own creation. Apparently it is adapted from a story by a guy named David Sedaris, in which his brother owns a bucket filled with candy because, "When shit brings you down, just say, 'Fuck it!' and eat yourself some fucking candy!"

I have seen it adapted to link with personal development. You can physically buy the bucket and throw things in it, or you can create a mental picture in your mind.

Thinking of doing something, but you have managed to think of every excuse why it won't work? Put it in the fuck-it bucket!

> "Your book will never be a success; nobody will buy it; you will look stupid!"

Self-limiting beliefs? Ahh, well – into the fuck-it bucket you go! Use it to fuel bravery!

The next time you start negative ruminating in your thoughts, and you can feel them spiralling, write down those thoughts, roll them into a ball and toss them into the bucket. Or alternatively, create that mental picture and just let them go.

Throw in those past disappointments you're holding on to and you want to let go. Allow yourself to do so.

People would argue that this is an irresponsible approach to life, and that's perhaps true on occasions, but it may just fuel that spark. Imagine some of the fears and worries you can let go of if you just choose to throw those doubts away.

Even if it isn't a long-term solution, at least you will have some fun in the process.

LIFE IS THE GOAL

In moving on from the previous section, we must also remember that life is the goal!

I once listened to a podcast called *The Positive Head*. One particular episode was listed as 'Life is the Goal', and it really got me thinking. It says our goals and ambitions are all in the future, when 'life' is right now. If we focus too much time on just chasing goals, then we may just miss life. Again, this was something I found interesting and again served as a reminder that it is all about finding balance. I do truly believe it is important to have goals and ambitions, but we must also take in life right now. This falls in line with *The Power of Now* discussed earlier but also with the work-life balance topic that is hotly discussed.

Using a hypothetical example, if you are a person who is working eighty plus hours a week on ensuring you become financially successful for your family, continually setting goals and achieving them, but as a result are missing your children grow up, to me you are missing life right now – this is my opinion. Successful sportspeople often tell their heroic stories of the effort they have put into achieving where they have got to, and it can be inspiring. However, we must find balance in life. For me, my midweek days are, for the most part, spent working full time, training, learning new skills or studying personal development, as well as writing this and working on my side business in my spare time. I am busy and I enjoy it. However, I always try to make an effort daily to sit down and have tea with my partner at night. Alternatively, it can be scheduling in time to make sure you spend it with important people, or simply find some time for enjoyment. On weekends I like to spend time doing the things I want to do, which can be something as simple as going camping or socialising. For me, it is so important; we don't know how long we have left and therefore it is critical that we enjoy every single moment we can in life. Not only this – it allows me to recharge and reset my batteries, and it also boosts my creativity.

I have seen it with many wealthy and 'successful' people. They are absolute high achievers and they smash their goals regularly, which is so inspiring. However, I have met many who are so unfulfilled in life. They have an abundance of wealth financially, but they are not finding the time to enjoy it. What is the fucking point? It must be balanced.

Don't get so caught up in worrying about the future that you fail to enjoy right now.

LIVE WITH PURPOSE

Remember, at the start, the abstract kept mentioning the word 'purpose'. Therefore, as I am drawing to a close of this book, I wanted to discuss the idea of living with purpose.

This is a concept that you can say has bugged the fucking life out of me. What I mean by this is… I honestly questioned, can we really live with a true purpose? Is it all a fairy tale?

I have read business books that have stated that we shouldn't search to find purpose and instead just look to make money. However, I have also read and heard much literature that states that we can find it, and we should always keep searching for it.

I have had friends tell me, "There is no purpose – we go to work to earn money, it's that simple," and, "Stop searching for purpose – just get on with life, purpose is unrealistic."

It was to the point where I thought that perhaps this was true, then. Perhaps if we are always looking for 'meaning' or 'purpose' to our lives, we may just never find it. It seemed like this unattainable, unrealistic, made-up construct.

Some people will believe that there is no such thing, and I completely respect that.

However, as I started to delve further into self-development and my growth journey – and, to some extent, as I reflected on what I have been doing with my life – it made me realise how promoting these messages now gives me a purpose. This is why I am choosing to pursue it.

I have struggled so much to find the right job, the right career. I have felt unfulfilled on a grand fucking scale; I have felt worthless and suffered a lot because of it. I questioned life as a whole. I have said to many people that what I was doing just wasn't truly for me. I knew I wanted more, but I was constantly met with this idea that what I was searching for just didn't exist. However, when I get engrossed in self-development, whether it's through reading or listening or writing this book, it gives me a true sense of joy.

I see all this work coming into fruition; it excites me that I may be able to help others. It's why I am pushing on so passionately with building my Joe Bloggs Talks brand. It is not for everyone, but for the people it does make a difference to, it matters.

I also got to the point where I genuinely believed I had no true passions in life anymore. As I have stated, I would often get fixated on things and then quickly lose interest (I still do with some things). This also helped start a loop of negative thoughts and would lead to vicious thought patterns and constantly questioning why I was doing things without having any real answers and a horrible feeling of low mood. However, with the self-development content, it's something I do daily and I do with genuine enjoyment.

I have a friend who is massively into photography. He

would often say to me things such as, "When I am taking photos, it makes me feel alive," and whilst I was absolutely thrilled for him, as I saw how much it meant to him, the other part of me was secretly hurting inside because I genuinely thought I would never find that.

Everything in life is part of our journey, and for me, this is starting to feel like a lot of my troubles have led me to down this route, to keep learning this stuff.

Some critics will also say that self-help is a load of shit – I also respect that, but for me, it has been life-changing.

Jumping back to the photography friend, credit where credit is due, he has taken that and taken it with both hands, all whilst working in a separate full-time job. He didn't let the opinion of others influence him. He didn't compare himself to others. He knew exactly what he wanted, and he has set out to achieve it.

Now I am not saying stop your job and decide you're going to be a photographer or an astronaut tomorrow, but if you want something and you truly believe it will add value to your life, then start taking steps to get there.

If you have not found your purpose yet, then do not give up on it! Keep searching for it. I am still working on myself every single day!

As well as this, being proactive is more likely to bring you opportunities than sitting still.

If you have found your purpose, then remind yourself about it daily. Keep being the best person that you can be. Keep striving and being a better version of yourself. If you take a step backwards, don't dwell, keep pushing forward… keep going and keep growing.

Steve Jobs famously said:

> "Your work is going to fill a large part of your life, and the only way to be truly satisfied is to do what you believe is great work. And the only way to do great work is to love what you do. If you haven't found it yet, keep looking. Don't settle. As with all matters of the heart, you'll know when you find it."

I reflect on careers a lot, but it is important to remember that purpose should not solely lie in the job we have. Perhaps your purpose is to be the best parent you can be, or something related to sport. The point I am trying to make is I feel the concept of purpose can be real. We just have to keep searching if we are not there yet. So many people are known to hit a realisation in later life where they feel they have just wasted themselves. This must be such a truly awful feeling.

Therefore, my next piece of advice is not to be afraid to be the person that you truly believe you are.

Dr Wayne Dyer makes a point to 'not die with your music still in you'. He goes on to say that all of us have some music playing, but too many of us are afraid to listen to that music and march to it. If there is something that you know you want to do, do not be afraid to go out and do it.

> "Whoever you are, whatever that music is, however distant it may sound, however strange, however weird others may interpret it to be — don't get to the end of your life and no, you're going to leave and not have it played yet, don't die with your music still in you."

This, to me, is fucking powerful. I know how shit it is to feel like you don't have that. I was once told I had a mid-life crisis before the age of twenty! And to some extent this could be true.

I must again stress, though, purpose does go beyond work. It applies to life in general, which is why I believe so strongly in setting goals. Set yourself challenges and work towards them. This gives you purpose every day, and whilst it may not be your 'life purpose', it always gives you something to strive towards. I think it's a huge contributor to living a fulfilling life.

FINAL TIPS AND ENDNOTES

THE MIND NEEDS CONSTANT DISCIPLINE

Self-development is a lifelong practice. The mind is a very powerful tool; this can be used to your advantage if you learn to control it and use it effectively.

The mind needs constant work to gain growth, and this requires discipline. If we stopped studying our competition in business, we would lose our edge; it is the same if we don't dedicate the time to nourish our minds.

Changes will not just happen for you; dedicate the time daily to focus on your mind. This could be breathing techniques or meditation, audiobooks or reading. Dedicate that time to feeding your mind with positive material and become conscious of what you are telling yourself.

You may have heard the saying 'change your mindset and change your life', and this is so true for me – it has genuinely made me a happier person, as well as being more motivated.

I don't always get everything right. You do not have to; it is unrealistic. Again, there is no such thing as 'life mastery'.

It would be hard to apply every single concept spoken about in here every single day; however, start applying some. Not every technique will work for you, but some will. Find out what works for you and be consistent with them every day.

Remember:

> "If nothing changes, nothing changes... you want change, make some."
>
> Courtney C. Stevens

I don't have a 'bulletproof' mindset; I am not claiming to be some elite-level thinker. I honestly just see myself as your typical, average guy who got sick of the same shit thoughts and feelings. I now truly recognise the value of working on my mindset. Make it one of the most fundamental parts of your life. You will thank yourself for it.

ENDNOTES

As we near a conclusion, I want you to realise that no matter what stage in life you are at, 'your story' is not over. You have the choice to change the course of your life at any given moment. We are never the finished product. We can never stop learning as individuals.

The truth is, life is not all hunky dory… life will throw us difficulties… we will have moments of immense sadness… we will lose loved ones… we will have days when we struggle… we will get stuck in traffic on the way to work… we will sometimes lose our job… some days we will meet a complete dickhead… but it's how we react to these situations that will often shape how we feel about life. I still have shit days now.

I know I always must always 'keep g(r)o(w)ing', and it gives me the courage to keep pushing forwards. I want to 'inspire and motivate change' for others.

If I feel stuck in something I am doing, I will search for answers.

Wherever you are now, you won't be there forever. Set goals and start giving yourself targets to achieve. Stay motivated and hungry.

If you are already killing life and feel content, keep working to be the optimum version of you.

Seriously, though, each morning you wake up, you get the opportunity to be the best you. You also get a completely new opportunity to change any way you want to or to certainly start working towards it. Make sure you seize it.

MENTAL HEALTH CONCLUDER

As I drew towards the end, I also wanted to speak specifically about the term 'mental health' for anyone who may be suffering with this. Again, I am not a trained professional on this, but because it has been real to me, I feel it is important to discuss.

On the *Headfirst* podcast by Joe O'Brien, he set out to answer the question, "Can I cure my mental health?"

Now, as he states, he does not like the word cure. However, he makes a very valid point, which resonated with me when I say we must work on our mental health daily. To me, this is now my personal development daily, which I have emphasised already.

He talks of our mental health being on a continuum, which, in a simplistic form, ranges from negative to positive.

He also makes the valid point that nobody is 'immune' from ill mental health.

He expresses how it is not black and white!

This resonates with me. People think that because you're

into 'self-development' or you're 'Mr Positive' now (which I have now been called — and I must say, that's slightly better than a miserable bastard or a drunk) that you don't have shit days. Believe me… you do!

The truth is, what makes us truly happy is different for everyone. I have just managed to find something for me that keeps me focused.

We must focus on feeling content and happy and fulfilled in life above everything else. As humans, we will always face trials and tribulations in life, as stated previously. We often hear upsetting stories about some of the tragic tales people have suffered as youngsters or tragic life events. The truth is, though, we also hear about people who overcame hardship and went on to live fulfilling lives. We can continue to find moments of joy, no matter how tough life may have been.

I wanted to end with something positive and that is that you're truly unique. This has cropped up in a number of self-development books I have read, and when you stop and give it some real thought, it is very powerful. Seriously, the chances of us even being born are estimated at one in four hundred trillion, and I have heard this number thrown around by many. That is fucking insane. It hurts my brain thinking about it!

The truth is, we don't know when life stops for us. Therefore, we should not waste our days wishing for others' lives, worrying about other people's opinions and getting worked up about any of the topics I have spoken about above. We do not get a second shot at this. Embrace everything about you. If you haven't found your passion yet, keep searching, keep working on you, keep striving for happiness and just do not give in. If you're loving life, keep on loving it.

MENTAL HEALTH CONCLUDER

Remember:

"You have a gift inside you, something unique to offer the world, no one else will be you."

Lewis Howes

FINAL NOTES

On a final note, thank you for reading. I hope you enjoyed it. If you got this far, you must have done. Or alternatively, you know me and you're just nosy ha-ha. I really do hope you took something from it.

This whole book served as a good daily reminder for me. It has served both as my counsellor but now my motivator and teacher at the same time. It has given me a purpose and focus but also fed positive material into my brain daily. I want you to find a way that does this for you too.

I am not done either! There is so much more I haven't even touched on yet; this is just the beginning of the Joe Bloggs Talks movement. I want to write a number of books and I want to use this as reflection tool.

Remember to keep striving for constant self-improvement. I once heard that you can have a PhD in any field, but learning about yourself is a number one priority. They do not teach this in schools, so be sure to instil it into your children from an early age.

Ask yourself, how can I improve today? How can I push

forwards? What can I be grateful for? As Tony Robbins says, ask yourself better questions and you will always get better answers.

This means that at the end of the day, you're not the same person that got out of bed and you're well on your way to being a better version of yourself. Winning.

If you want any more positive material, don't forget to check out www.joebloggstalks.com for my blog. You can also find 'Joe Bloggs Talks' on Facebook (business page and positive community group) as well as Instagram. I also have a podcast I run with a friend, titled *Joe Bloggs Talks*, in which we interview guests with inspiring stories and give our own motivating advice. We also have a YouTube channel.

The thing is, I don't see myself as anything special. I am your average Joe, your Joe Bloggs, who just managed to find a passion and taught myself the principles in this book. We all can use them. My message is to encourage as many people in the world to use them too.

CONCLUDING ALL PIECES OF GUIDANCE

As a final summary, below are my summarised points for living a better life and how to consistently improve as a person.

Negative thoughts seriously have the potential to give you a lifetime of unhappiness. Nobody wants that! It is up to you to take action. If you don't do something about it, it has the potential to follow you wherever you go. I am also going to use the below as my positive reminder when I am having a shit day myself.

- Carry a journal.
- Engage in self-development *daily*.
- Being 'stuck' needs to be used for positive change.
- Find your 'why' – it is your driving force.
- Aim for fulfilment.
- Let go of the opinions of others. You're wasting your energy.
- If you want change, then you have to change.
- Everything comes down to our decisions.

CONCLUDING ALL PIECES OF GUIDANCE

- Stop comparing yourself to others it will make you unhappy – find a role model instead.
- Direct your thoughts more positively.
- Use positive language more and perform positive affirmations to help.
- Stop with negative ruminations – take your finger out the fucking fire.
- Stop limiting yourself with your beliefs.
- Stop worrying over shit you cannot control.
- Try to focus on the 'now' more and don't get stuck regretting the past or worrying about the future.
- Never stop learning, but don't be a know it all.
- Have the right mindset to learning.
- Feed yourself with positive learning such as audiobooks, podcasts and books.
- Start journaling and capture your ideas.
- Jot down negative emotions to turn them into solutions.
- Be your own counsellor if you need to be.
- Be the best version of yourself.
- Write down inspiring quotes/mantra to motivate you.
- Be nice to one another and stop being a dick for no reason.
- Start smiling more and say hello to strangers.
- You can change your state or focus if you are having a shit day.
- Get rid of negative people they serve you no purpose, or choose how you respond to them.
- Limit your intake of the news and media, or at least the depressing stuff.
- Surround yourself with positive people (they're better for you).

- Be grateful for the things you have.
- Let go of past mistakes – they don't serve you well.
- Try to let go of resentment – it is only hurting you.
- Learn to forgive yourself.
- Learn to love yourself; you spend a lot of time with yourself, so make it good.
- Do not be afraid to ask for help – it isn't a weakness.
- Set goals, draw a vision board and take action.
- Create positive habits.
- Get into a morning routine – it will give you more free time and set you up for the day.
- Get rid of the fear of failure – it's not serving you.
- Journal.
- Get outdoors more or simply have more fun – it's good for you.
- Put down your phone when having dinner – use it for positive things only.
- Spend time with loved ones and make a call to someone you haven't spoken to in a while.
- Get as social as you can.
- Slow down.
- Change your perception of life itself – not everything has to be gloomy.
- Remember life is a big experiment.
- If all else fails, throw it in the 'fuck-it' bucket.
- Whilst chasing goals, don't forget to live now.
- Keep chasing your purpose if you haven't found it yet. Give yourself something purposeful to work for each day.
- The mind needs constant work and attention – therefore, do not neglect it.